Comprehensive Cybersecurity Handbook for Novice Readers

Introduction to Cybersecurity

Krasimir Vatchinsky

CONTENTS

I. AN INTRODUCTION TO CYBERSECURITY

What is Cybersecurity?

Also known as information security or IT security, is a multidisciplinary field that focuses on protecting computer systems, networks, programs, and data from unauthorized access, attacks, damage, or exploitation.

Cybersecurity encompasses a range of technologies, processes, and practices designed to safeguard digital information and ensure the confidentiality, integrity, and availability of computing resources. The goal of cybersecurity is to safeguard against a wide range of threats, including hacking attempts, malware, phishing, and other cyberattacks.

Let review the key components of cybersecurity:

1. **Network Security:** involves protecting network infrastructure, including routers, switches, firewalls, and other devices, to prevent unauthorized access and secure data transmission.

2. **Firewalls:** provide a barrier between a trusted internal network and untrustworthy external networks, controlling both incoming and outgoing network traffic.

3. **Intrusion Detection Systems (IDS) and Intrusion Prevention Systems (IPS):** monitor network or system activities for malicious exploits or security policy violations.

4. **Endpoint Security:** This component focuses on securing individual devices, such as computers, laptops, and mobile phones. Endpoint security measures include antivirus software, firewalls, and intrusion detection systems.

5. **Antivirus Software:** protects endpoints (such as computers and mobile devices) from malicious software by detecting and removing viruses, malware, and other threats.

6. **Endpoint Detection and Response (EDR):** Monitor and respond to advanced threats on endpoints in real-time.

7. **Application Security:** This component should protect software applications from potential threats and vulnerabilities. Application security includes secure coding practices, regular testing, and software patching to mitigate vulnerabilities.

8. **Secure Coding Practices:** involves writing code with security in mind to prevent vulnerabilities that attackers could exploit.

9. **Web Application Firewalls (WAF):** protects web applications from various attacks, such as SQL injection, cross-site scripting (XSS), and other common vulnerabilities.

10. **Cloud Security:** with the increasing use of cloud computing, this component allows for cybersecurity extends to protect data and applications stored in cloud environments. This includes implementing access controls, encryption, and monitoring for cloud services.

11. **Cloud Access Security Brokers (CASB):** provides security policy enforcement between users and cloud applications.

12. **Secure Configuration:** ensures that the IT team securely configures cloud services and infrastructure to prevent vulnerabilities.

13. **Identity and Access Management (IAM):** this component involves managing and controlling user access to systems and data. IAM includes authentication, authorization, and identity

verification processes to ensure that only authorized individuals have access to sensitive information.

14. **Authentication:** verifies the identity of users or systems through methods like passwords, multi-factor authentication, biometrics, or digital certificates.

15. **Authorization:** controls access to resources based on the authenticated user's permissions and role.

16. **Data Security:** this component focuses on protecting the confidentiality and integrity of data. This involves encryption, data loss prevention (DLP), and secure data storage practices.

17. **Encryption:** this component converts sensitive data into unreadable code to prevent unauthorized access. This is crucial for protecting data during transmission and storage.

18. **Data Loss Prevention (DLP):** monitors and controls data transfer to prevent unauthorized access and ensure compliance with security policies.

19. **Incident Response and Management:** this component, the ability to detect on-time and respond to cybersecurity incidents, is crucial. Incident response plans outline the steps to be taken in case of a security breach.

20. **Cybersecurity Incident Response Plan (CIRP):** defines the steps to be taken when a cybersecurity incident occurs, helping to minimize damage and recover it without network downtime delay.

21. **Forensics:** collects, analysis, and preservation of digital evidence to understand and respond to security incidents.

22. **Security Awareness and Training:** this component educating employees and users about cybersecurity guideline is essential. This includes raising awareness about phishing attacks, social engineering, and other common threats.

23. **Employee Training:** ensures that individuals within an organization are aware of cybersecurity guideline and potential threats.

24. **Phishing Awareness:** educates users about the risks of phishing attacks and how to recognize and avoid them.

25. **Physical Security:** this component refers to the measures and strategies implemented to safeguard physical assets, people, and resources from unauthorized access, damage, theft, or harm. It involves the use of physical barriers, access controls, surveillance systems, and security personnel to protect facilities, infrastructure, and information systems.

    The primary goal of physical security is to create a secure environment that prevents or mitigates physical threats and ensures the safety and integrity of an organization's tangible assets. In conclusion, physical security measures often complement digital security practices to create a comprehensive security framework for overall protection.

26. **Access Control Systems:** restricts physical access to data centers, server rooms, and other critical infrastructures.

27. **Surveillance Systems:** monitors physical spaces to detect and deter unauthorized access.

II. LATEST TRENDS IN CYBERSECURITY

1. Zero Trust Security Model: this component approach assumes that no one, even those inside the organization's network, should be trusted. All access needs to be granted based on verification and authentication.

The Zero Trust Security Model is a cybersecurity approach that challenges the traditional notion of trust within an organizational network. In a traditional security model, once a user gains access to the internal network, there's a tendency to trust their activities and movements within that network.

In conclusion, the Zero Trust model operates on the principle of "never trust, always verify," assuming that no entity, whether internal or external, should be trusted automatically.

Let's review the key components and principles of the Zero Trust Security Model:

1.1. Zero Trust Architecture:

- Micro-Segmentation: this component divides the network into smaller, isolated segments, making it more difficult for attackers to move laterally within the network. Each segment requires separate authentication and authorization.

- **Least Privilege Access:** all users and systems are granted the minimum level of access necessary to perform their tasks, reducing the potential impact of a security breach.

1.2. Identity-Centric Security:

- **Identity Verification:** emphasizes identity as the new perimeter, requiring strong authentication methods, such as multi-factor authentication (MFA) to verify the identity of users and devices.

- **Continuous Authentication:** rather than a onetime authentication, continuous monitoring of user behavior and access patterns helps detect anomalies and potential security threats.

1.3. Device Security:

- **Device Trustworthiness:** ensures that devices connecting to the network are secure and compliant with security policies before granting access.

- **Endpoint Protection:** uses endpoint security solutions to protect devices from malware and other threats.

1.4. Network Security:

- **Network Visibility:** a comprehensive understanding of all devices, users, and activities on the network is crucial for effective security monitoring and response.

- **Encrypted Traffic Inspection:** analyzes encrypted traffic to detect and prevent malicious activities that may be hidden within the encrypted communication.

1.5. Application Security:

- **Secure Access to Applications:** access to applications is restricted and granted based on user identity, device trustworthiness, and the principle of least privilege.

- **Application Layer Security:** ensures that applications are securely developed, deployed, and configured to minimize vulnerabilities.

1.6. Continuous Monitoring and Analytics:

- **Behavioral Analysis:** continuously monitors user and system behavior to detect deviations from normal patterns that may show potential security threats.

- **Real-time Incident Response:** enables swift response to security incidents in real time as they were identified, reducing the impact of a breach.

1.7. Policy Enforcement:

- **Dynamic Policy Enforcement:** all security policies need to be dynamically adjusted based on the changing security landscape, user behavior, and contextual information.

- **Automation and Orchestration:** leverages automation to enforce policies and respond to security events in real-time.

1.8. Data Security:

- **Data Encryption and Tokenization:** protect sensitive data by encrypting it during transmission and storage or by using tokenization techniques.

- **Data Loss Prevention (DLP):** monitors and controls data transfer to prevent unauthorized access and data leakage.

In conclusion, implementing a Zero Trust Security Model requires a holistic and adaptive approach that considers the dynamic nature of today's cybersecurity landscape.

This security model helps organizations enhance their security posture by minimizing the attack surface and providing a more robust defense against growing threats.

2. AI and Machine Learning in Cybersecurity: supporting artificial intelligence and machine learning for threat detection and response is becoming prevalent. These new technologies help in identifying patterns and anomalies that may reveal a potential security threat.

AI (Artificial Intelligence) and Machine Learning (ML) play a crucial role in enhancing cybersecurity by providing advanced capabilities for threat detection, response, and overall security management.

Let's review their roles in cybersecurity:

2.1. Threat Detection and Prevention:

- **Anomaly Detection:** AI and ML algorithms analyze normal patterns of user behavior, network traffic, and system activities. All deviations from these patterns can be identified as anomalies, showing potentially malicious activities.

- **Behavioral Analytics:** ML models learn the typical behavior of users and systems, enabling the detection of abnormal or suspicious activities that may show a security threat.

2.2. Endpoint Security:

- **Malware Detection:** ML algorithms can identify patterns associated with malware by analyzing file characteristics, behavior, and code. This aids in the active detection and prevention of malware at endpoints.

- **Endpoint Protection Platforms (EPP):** AI-driven EPP solutions provide real-time protection by constantly learning and adapting to emerging threats.

2.3. Network Security:

- **Intrusion Detection and Prevention Systems (IDPS):** ML enhances the ability to identify and respond to network intrusions by learning from historical data and recognizing patterns associated with different types of hacking attacks.

- **Traffic Analysis:** ML algorithms analyze network traffic to identify unusual patterns or malicious activities, helping to detect and prevent attacks such as DDoS (Distributed Denial of Service).

2.4. User Authentication and Access Control:

- **Behavior-Based Authentication:** ML models analyze user behavior, such as typing patterns and mouse movements, to establish a baseline for normal user activity. Deviations from this baseline can trigger additional authentication measures.

- **Access Policies:** ML helps define and adjusting access policies based on user behavior and contextual information, ensuring that access privileges align with current security requirements.

2.5. Incident Response and Forensics:

- **Automated Incident Response:** ML algorithms can automate certain aspects of incident response by rapidly analyzing and correlating large volumes of data to identify and mitigate security incidents.

- **Forensic Analysis:** ML aids in forensic investigations by analyzing massive datasets to identify patterns and indicators of compromise, helping security teams understand the scope and impact of an incident.

2.6. Phishing and Social Engineering Detection:

- **Email Security:** ML algorithms analyze email content, sender behavior, and other attributes to identify phishing attempts and malicious emails.

- **User Awareness Training:** ML can personalize and optimize security awareness training programs based on individual user vulnerabilities and learning patterns.

2.7. Security Operations and Management:

- **Security Information and Event Management (SIEM):** ML enhances SIEM capabilities by automating the analysis of log data, correlating events, and identifying patterns indicative of security incidents.

- **Threat Intelligence:** ML helps in processing and analyzing large volumes of threat intelligence data to identify emerging threats and update security measures accordingly.

2.8. Adversarial Machine Learning (AML):

- **Defense Against Adversarial Attacks:** as attackers may attempt to manipulate ML models, AML techniques focus on making ML models more robust against adversarial attempts to deceive or manipulate them.

2.9. Risk Assessment and Prediction:

- **Predictive Analytics:** ML models analyze historical data to predict potential future security threats and vulnerabilities, allowing organizations to proactively address and mitigate risks.

- **Vulnerability Management:** ML aids in identifying and prioritizing vulnerabilities based on the potential impact and likelihood of exploitation.

2.10. Automated Threat Hunting:

- **Automated Threat Detection:** ML-driven tools assist security analysts in proactively hunting for threats by analyzing data and identifying patterns that may go unnoticed through manual analysis.

In conclusion, integrating AI and ML in cybersecurity empowers organizations to stay ahead of growing threats, automate routine tasks, and enhance the overall effectiveness of security measures.

These technologies contribute significantly to creating a more adaptive and resilient cybersecurity infrastructure.

3. IoT Security: as the number of Internet of Things (IoT) devices continues to grow, securing these interconnected devices becomes critical to prevent potential vulnerabilities and cyberattacks. The IoT (Internet of Things) security is a critical aspect of cybersecurity that focuses on protecting the vast and diverse network of interconnected devices, sensors, and systems that make up the IoT ecosystem.

Because of proliferating IoT devices in various industries, securing these devices is essential to prevent potential vulnerabilities and mitigate the risks associated with unauthorized access and data breaches.

Let's review the key aspects of IoT security:

3.1. Device Authentication and Identity Management:

- **Unique Identifiers:** each IoT device should have a unique identifier to ensure that only allowed devices can connect to the network.

- **Secure Authentication Protocols:** implement strong authentication mechanisms such as certificate-based authentication to verify the identity of devices before granting access.

3.2. Data Encryption and Privacy:

- **End-to-End Encryption:** encrypt data both in transit and at rest to protect sensitive information from eavesdropping and unauthorized access.

- **Data Minimization:** collect and store only the necessary data, reducing the potential impact of a security breach.

3.3. Network Security:

- **Segmentation:** isolate IoT devices into separate network segments to contain potential security breaches and limit lateral movement within the network.

- **Firewalls and Intrusion Detection Systems:** implement network security measures to monitor and control traffic, detect anomalies, and prevent unauthorized access.

3.4. Secure Firmware and Software Updates:

- **Code Signing:** ensure that firmware and software updates are signed with digital signatures to verify their authenticity.
- **Secure Over-the-Air (OTA) Updates:** implement secure channels for updating device firmware and software to prevent unauthorized modifications.

3.5. Physical Security:

- **Tamper Detection:** incorporates mechanisms to detect physical tampering with IoT devices, triggering alerts or disabling the device in case of unauthorized access.

- **Secure Boot:** ensure that only authenticated and unaltered firmware is loaded during the device boot process.

3.6. Device Lifecycle Management:

- **Inventory and Asset Management:** maintain an inventory of all IoT devices, including details about their configurations and software versions.

- **Device Decommissioning:** develop processes for securely decommissioning and retiring IoT devices to prevent lingering security risks.

3.7. IoT Protocols and Standards:

- **Secure Protocols:** use secure communication protocols (e.g., MQTT over TLS) to protect data exchanged between IoT devices and the cloud.

- **Compliance with Standards:** adhere to industry-accepted security standards and guidelines to ensure a consistent and robust security posture.

3.8. Edge Computing Security:

- **Security at the Edge:** implement security measures on edge devices to protect sensitive data processed locally.

- **Edge Authentication:** secure communication between IoT devices and edge computing nodes with strong authentication mechanisms.

3.9. Supply Chain Security:

- **Vendor Assessment:** evaluate the security practices of IoT device vendors, including their development processes and adherence to security standards.

- **Secure Manufacturing Processes:** ensure that devices are securely manufactured, preventing introducing vulnerabilities during the production process.

3.10. User Education and Awareness:

- **End-User Training:** educate end-users about the security risks associated with IoT devices and provide guidance on guidelines for securing and using these devices.

- **Default Credential Management:** encourage users to change default usernames and passwords on IoT devices to prevent unauthorized access.

3.11. Regulatory Compliance:

- Compliance with Data Protection Laws: ensure that IoT deployments comply with relevant data protection and privacy regulations, considering the sensitive nature of IoT data.

IoT security requires a comprehensive and multi-layered approach to address the unique challenges posed by the diverse range of devices in the IoT ecosystem.

By implementing robust security measures helps organizations build a resilient and secure IoT infrastructure.

4. Ransomware Defense: with the rise of ransomware attacks, organizations are focusing on robust backup and recovery strategies, as well as implementing advanced threat detection to combat this specific type of cyber threat.

Ransomware defense is a critical aspect of cybersecurity that focuses on preventing, detecting, and responding to ransomware attacks. Ransomware is a type of malicious software that encrypts a victim's files or systems and demands payment (usually in cryptocurrency) for the release of the decryption key. An effective ransomware defense involves mix preventive measures, user education, and incident response strategies.

Let's review the key components of ransomware defense:

4.1. User Training and Awareness:

- **Phishing Awareness:** educate users about the risks of phishing attacks, as many ransomware incidents start with phishing emails. Teach them to recognize suspicious emails, links, and attachments.

- **Social Engineering Awareness:** users should be mindful of social engineering tactics used by attackers to manipulate them into taking actions that may lead to a ransomware infection.

4.2. Regular Backups and Data Recovery:

- **Backup Policies:** implement regular and automated backup procedures for critical data. Ensure that all backups are stored offline or in isolated environments to prevent them from being compromised during an attack.

- **Testing Backups:** regularly test the restoration process to verify the integrity of backups and the organization's ability to recover data in case of a ransomware incident.

4.3. Endpoint Protection:

- **Antivirus and Anti-Malware Solutions:** employ robust endpoint security solutions that include real-time scanning and heuristic analysis to detect and block ransomware.

- **Endpoint Detection and Response (EDR):** use EDR solutions to monitor endpoint activities, detect suspicious behavior, and respond to threats in real-time.

4.4. Network Security:

- **Firewalls and Intrusion Prevention Systems (IPS):** configure firewalls and IPS to block malicious traffic and prevent ransomware from spreading within the network.

- **Segmentation:** implement network segmentation to isolate critical systems and limit lateral movement in case of a ransomware infection.

4.5. Email Security:

- **Email Filtering:** employ advanced email filtering solutions to block malicious attachments and links in emails, reducing the likelihood of users falling victim to phishing or downloading ransomware.

4.6. Patch Management:

- **Regular Updates:** keep operating systems, software, and applications up to date with the latest security patches to address known vulnerabilities that ransomware could exploit.
- **Vulnerability Scanning:** conduct regular vulnerability assessments to identify and remediate potential weaknesses in the IT infrastructure.

4.7. User Privilege Management:

- **Least Privilege Principle:** limit user access rights to the minimum necessary for their job responsibilities. This reduces the impact of a ransomware infection by restricting the attacker's ability to move laterally within the network.

4.8. Incident Response Plan:

- **Develop a Plan:** create a comprehensive incident response plan that outlines the steps to be taken in the event of a ransomware attack.

- **Tabletop Exercises:** conduct regular tabletop exercises to test the incident response plan and ensure that personnel are familiar with their roles and responsibilities.

4.9. Threat Intelligence:

- **Monitoring Threat Intelligence Feeds:** stay informed about the latest ransomware threats and tactics through threat intelligence feeds. Use this information to enhance security measures and update detection capabilities.

4.10. Security Awareness Training for Employees:

- **Simulated Attacks:** conduct simulated ransomware attacks to train employees on how to respond and report potential incidents.

- **Regular Training Updates:** keep employees informed about growing ransomware tactics and strategies for staying vigilant.

4.11. Legal and Regulatory Compliance:

- **Compliance Checks:** ensure that the organization's ransomware defense measures align with legal and regulatory requirements, especially those related to data protection and incident reporting.

4.12. Engagement with Law Enforcement:

- **Collaboration with Authorities:** establish relationships with law enforcement agencies and cybersecurity authorities to facilitate information sharing and collaboration in the event of a ransomware incident.

Ransomware defense requires a holistic and active approach that combines technical controls, user education, and preparedness for rapid response. By implementing a comprehensive defense strategy, organizations can reduce the risk of falling victim to ransomware and minimize the potential impact of such attacks.

5. 5G Security: As 5G networks roll out, there is a heightened focus on ensuring securing these high-speed, low-latency networks to prevent potential cyber threats and attacks. 5G security is a critical aspect of ensuring the safe and resilient deployment of fifth generation (5G) mobile networks.

As 5G technology becomes more widespread, it brings many benefits, such as increased data speeds, low latency, and the ability to connect a vast number of devices simultaneously. However, with these advantages comes the need for robust security measures to address potential vulnerabilities and safeguard against various cyber threats.

Let's review the key components of 5G security:

5.1. Network Slicing Security:

- **Isolation of Slices:** 5G allows for network slicing, where virtual networks with unique characteristics can be created. Security mechanisms must ensure the isolation and integrity of these slices to prevent cross-slice attacks.

5.2. Authentication and Identity Management:

- **Subscriber Identity Privacy:** implement techniques designed to protect subscriber identities and maintain user privacy, such as using temporary identifiers and pseudonyms.

- **Strong Authentication:** enhance authentication mechanisms, including the use of multi-factor authentication, to secure access to 5G networks and services.

5.3. Secure Signaling:

- **Security in Control Plane Signaling:** ensure securing signaling messages in the control plane to prevent attacks on network functions and services.

- **Protection Against Spoofing:** implement measures to detect and prevent signaling message spoofing and manipulation.

5.4. Encryption and Integrity Protection:

- **End-to-End Encryption:** employ strong encryption protocols to protect data both in transit and at rest, ensuring the confidentiality and integrity of communications.

- **Integrity Verification:** implement mechanisms to verify the integrity of transmitted data and detect any tampering attempts.

5.5. Virtualization Security:

- **Security of Virtual Network Functions (VNFs):** ensure securing virtualized network functions through measures such as hypervisor security, secure bootstrapping, and secure deployment practices.

- **Isolation Between Virtualized Resources:** maintain strong isolation between virtualized resources to prevent unauthorized access and lateral movement within virtualized environments.

5.6. Edge Computing Security:

- **Security at the Edge:** implement security measures for edge computing nodes to protect against potential attacks on applications and services deployed at the network edge.

- **Secure APIs:** ensure that APIs (Application Programming Interfaces) used in edge computing environments are secure and not vulnerable to exploitation.

5.7. User Equipment (UE) Security:

- **Device Security:** ensure that user devices (e.g., smartphones, IoT devices) connecting to 5G networks are secure and free from malware.

- **UE Authentication:** implement strong authentication mechanisms for user equipment to prevent unauthorized access.

5.8. Network Function Security:

- **Security of Network Elements:** secure network functions such as base stations, core network elements, and network management systems against potential attacks, ensuring their resilience.

- **API Security:** protect APIs used for communication between network functions to prevent unauthorized access and data manipulation.

5.9. Security Monitoring and Incident Response:

- **Real-time Monitoring:** implement real-time monitoring of network traffic, activities, and events to detect anomalies and potential security incidents.

- **Incident Response Plan:** develop and test regularly an incident response plan to ensure a swift and coordinated response to security breaches.

5.10. Regulatory Compliance:

- **Compliance Checks:** ensure that 5G deployments adhere to relevant regulatory and industry-specific security standards and requirements.

- **Privacy Regulations:** address privacy considerations and comply with data protection regulations applicable to 5G networks and services.

5.11. Supply Chain Security:

- **Vendor Risk Management:** assess and manage security risks associated with 5G equipment and infrastructure providers.

- **Secure Manufacturing Processes:** Ensure securing hardware and software components throughout the supply chain to prevent introducing vulnerabilities.

5.12. Threat Intelligence Sharing:

- **Collaboration with Industry Partners:** engage in information sharing and collaboration with other telecommunication providers, industry partners, and cybersecurity organizations to stay informed about emerging threats and vulnerabilities.

In conclusion, by addressing these aspects of 5G security, telecommunication providers and organizations can create a robust and resilient environment that safeguards the integrity, confidentiality, and availability of 5G networks and services.

This multi-faceted approach is crucial for building trust in the deployment and adoption of 5G technology.

6. Quantum Computing Threats: With developing quantum computers, there are concerns about their potential to break existing encryption algorithms, prompting the need for quantum-resistant cryptographic solutions. Quantum computing, while holding tremendous potential for solving complex problems at speeds unattainable by classical computers, also introduces new security threats that can affect current cryptographic systems.

As quantum computers advance, they may compromise extensively used encryption algorithms, posing risks to the confidentiality and integrity of sensitive information.

Let's review the key quantum computing threats:

6.1. Shor's Algorithm and RSA Cryptography:

- **Factorization of Large Numbers:** Shor's algorithm, a quantum algorithm, has the potential to efficiently factor large numbers, challenging the security of widely used public-key cryptosystems like RSA.

- **RSA Vulnerability:** quantum computers with sufficient qubits could efficiently factorize the large semi-prime numbers used in RSA, breaking the security of communications encrypted with RSA algorithms.

6.2. Elliptic Curve Cryptography (ECC) Threats:

- **Discrete Logarithm Problem:** quantum computers can efficiently solve the discrete logarithm problem, which is the basis of ECC. This puts elliptic curve cryptography, widely used for its efficiency, at risk.

- **ECC Vulnerability:** quantum computers might break ECC-based encryption, affecting the security of the systems relying on elliptic curve cryptography.

6.3. Grover's Algorithm and Hash Functions:

- **Search Algorithms:** Grover's algorithm provides a quadratic speedup for unstructured search problems, including hash function inversion.

- **Cryptographic Hash Function Vulnerability:** Grover's algorithm reduces the security strength of hash functions, requiring longer hash lengths for equivalent classical security levels.

6.4. Quantum Key Distribution (QKD) Vulnerabilities:

- Quantum Channel Attacks: quantum key distribution relies on the principles of quantum mechanics to secure communication channels. However, certain physical implementations may be vulnerable to quantum channel attacks.

- Technological Challenges: practical deployment of QKD systems faces challenges such as distance limitations, key distribution rates, and susceptibility to side-channel attacks.

6.5. Post-Quantum Cryptography Transition:

- Algorithm Migration: as quantum computers advance, there is a need to transition to post-quantum cryptographic algorithms that are believed to be secure against quantum attacks.

- Interim Security Measures: organizations need to adopt interim security measures to protect existing data until post-quantum cryptographic solutions are standardized and widely implemented.

6.6. Quantum-Safe Cryptography Adoption:

- Industry Readiness: organizations may lag in adopting quantum-safe cryptographic algorithms, leading to potential vulnerabilities in systems relying on classical cryptographic methods.

- Global Standards: establishing global standards for quantum-safe cryptography is crucial to ensure interoperability and robust security across diverse systems.

6.7. Multivariate Polynomial Cryptography Risks:

- Vulnerability to Quantum Algorithms: certain multivariate polynomial cryptographic schemes, while considered secure against classical attacks, may become vulnerable to quantum algorithms.

- Algorithmic Exploration: researchers need to explore and develop quantum-resistant variants of cryptographic algorithms, including multivariate polynomial schemes.

6.8. Quantum Cloud Security Concerns:

- **Outsourcing Risks:** Organizations relying on quantum computing services from cloud providers may face risks if providers are compromised, affecting the confidentiality of quantum computations.

- **Data Privacy:** the nature of quantum computations raises concerns about data privacy, especially when dealing with sensitive information in a cloud-based quantum computing environment.

6.9. Quantum Random Number Generators (QRNG) Security:

- **Randomness Assurance:** quantum random number generators are susceptible to certain attacks, and ensuring the integrity of quantum-generated randomness is essential for cryptographic applications.

- **Secure QRNG Implementation:** robust implementation and validation of quantum random number generators are critical for maintaining the security of cryptographic systems.

6.10. Quantum-Specific Threats to Cryptographic Protocols:

- **Quantum Attacks on Protocols:** quantum computers may introduce a new type of attacks specific to cryptographic protocols, requiring a reassessment of the security of existing protocols.

- **Quantum Cryptanalysis Research:** continuous research is required to understand potential quantum-specific threats and vulnerabilities in cryptographic protocols.

As quantum computing technology progresses, addressing these threats requires a concerted effort from the cryptographic community, industry stakeholders, and standardization bodies. Preparing for the post-quantum era involves developing and adopting quantum-resistant cryptographic algorithms, implementing secure transition strategies, and ensuring the resilience of information systems against emerging quantum threats.

In conclusion, cybersecurity is a dynamic and growing field that plays a crucial role in safeguarding our progressively digitalized world. Staying informed about the latest trends and implementing strong security measures is essential for effective protection against cyber threats.

III. HACKING

Hacking is the unauthorized access, manipulation, or exploitation of computer systems, networks, or data. While the term "hacker" had a positive connotation referring to skilled programmers, it has grown to include individuals or groups with malicious intent. Hacking activities can range from a harmless exploration of systems (ethical hacking) to malicious actions aimed at stealing sensitive information, disrupting operations, or causing damage.

1. Commonalities and Differences:

1.1. Intent:

- **Cybersecurity:** aims to protect and secure systems, networks, and data from unauthorized access and cyber threats.

- **Hacking:** involves attempting to compromise the security of the systems, often with malicious intent.

1.2. Methods:

- **Cybersecurity:** involves implementing preventive measures, such as firewalls, encryption, and access controls, to defend against cyber threats.

- **Hacking:** encompasses a variety of techniques, including exploiting vulnerabilities, conducting social engineering attacks, and using malware to gain unauthorized access.

1.3.   Ethical Considerations:

- **Cybersecurity:** mostly is focused on ethical and legal practices to protect digital assets and maintain the integrity of systems.

- **Hacking:** unethical hacking involves actions that violate laws and ethical standards, posing a threat to individuals, organizations, and society at large.

2.   Latest Information:

2.1.   Ethical Hacking and Bug Bounty Programs:

- Organizations are recognizing the value of ethical hacking to identify vulnerabilities before malicious hackers can exploit them. Bug bounty programs reward ethical hackers to discover and report security flaws.

2.2.   Advanced Persistent Threats (APTs):

- APTs are sophisticated and targeted cyberattacks often associated with nation-state actors. Cybersecurity professionals are focusing on advanced threat detection and response to mitigate the impact of APTs.

2.3.   Ransomware and Extortion:

- Ransomware attacks continue to rise, with cybercriminals targeting individuals, businesses, and even critical infrastructure. Prevention strategies include robust backup solutions and cybersecurity awareness training.

2.4.   Zero-Day Vulnerabilities:

- The discovery and exploitation of zero-day vulnerabilities (unpatched software vulnerabilities) remain a significant concern. Cybersecurity experts work on rapid detection and mitigation of these vulnerabilities.

2.5.   AI-Driven Cybersecurity Solutions:

- Integrating artificial intelligence (AI) and machine learning in cybersecurity solutions enhances threat detection capabilities by identifying patterns and anomalies in large datasets.

2.6.   Supply Chain Security:

- There is an increased focus on securing the supply chain, as cyber attackers often target vulnerabilities in third-party software or services to gain access to the target organization.

In summary, while cybersecurity is an active and ethical approach to safeguarding digital assets, hacking encompasses a broad range of activities, some of which are with malicious intent and illegal. The growing landscape requires continuous efforts to stay ahead of emerging threats and adopt advanced cybersecurity measures. Ethical hacking practices and collaboration between cybersecurity professionals and the wider community are essential in the ongoing battle against cyber threats.

.

IV COMMON TYPES OF CYBER ATTACKS

Experts categorize cybersecurity threats into different types based on their nature and characteristics. Two common categories are "Passive Threats" and "Active Threats."

Let's explore these categories and how specific threats fall into each:

1. Passive Threats:

Passive threats involve unauthorized access or disclosure of information without actively disrupting the system. While they may not directly cause harm, they can compromise the confidentiality of sensitive data.

1.1. Passive Eavesdropping:

Description: Unauthorized interception of communication to listen in on sensitive information.

Nature: Passive

Method of Protection:

- Encryption: use end-to-end encryption to secure communication channels.

- Secure Communication Protocols: employ secure protocols such as HTTPS.

- Real-life Example: The Edward Snowden revelations in 2013 exposed global surveillance programs where intelligence agencies were accused of eavesdropping on electronic communications, leading to concerns about privacy.

1.2.   Traffic Analysis:

Description: Monitoring and analyzing patterns in communication to gain insights into activities.

Nature: Passive

Method of Protection:

- Traffic Encryption: encrypt data to prevent analysis.

- Anonymization Techniques: mask data to obscure patterns.

- Real-life Example: In 2014, researchers showed how metadata collected from mobile phones could be used for traffic analysis, revealing users' movements and interactions without accessing the actual content of the communications.

1.3.   Data Mining:

Description: Extracting valuable information from large datasets without disrupting the system.

Nature: Passive

Method of Protection:

- Data Encryption: protect sensitive data with encryption.

- Access Controls: implement strict access controls to limit data exposure.

- Real-life Example: The Cambridge Analytica scandal in 2018 involved the unauthorized mining of Facebook user data for political advertising, raising concerns about the misuse of personal information.

1.4.   Social Engineering:

Description: Manipulating individuals to divulge confidential information through psychological tactics.

Nature: Can be both passive and active, depending on the approach.

Method of Protection:
- Security Awareness Training: Educate users about social engineering tactics.

- Two-Factor Authentication (2FA): Add an extra layer of authentication to prevent unauthorized access.

- Real-life Example: a phishing attack, where attackers tricked individuals into revealing email credentials, leading to sensitive information exposure facilitated The 2016 DNC email leak.

2. Active Threats:

Active threats involve actions that directly disrupt or compromise the integrity and availability of systems and data.

2.1.   Malware:

Description: malicious software that actively harms systems, steals data, or disrupts normal operations.

Nature: Active

Methods of Protection:

- Antivirus Software: regularly update and use antivirus tools.

- User Education: train users to avoid downloading and executing unknown files.

- Real-life Example: The NotPetya ransomware attack in 2017 affected companies worldwide, encrypting data and demanding ransom payments. It was later revealed to be destructive wiper malware disguised as ransomware.

2.2.   Phishing:

Description: social engineering attack actively attempting to deceive individuals into divulging sensitive information.

Nature: Active

Methods of Protection:

- Email Filtering: implement email filters to detect and block phishing emails.

- User Training: educate users about recognizing phishing attempts.

- Real-life Example: The 2016 Gmail phishing attack targeted Google users by tricking them into clicking on a malicious link, leading to compromised accounts and unauthorized access.

2.3.   Ransomware:

Description: actively encrypts files or systems and demands payment for decryption.

Nature: Active

Methods of Protection:

- Regular Backups: ensure data backups are regularly performed and stored securely.

- Security Software: use robust security solutions to detect and prevent ransomware.

- Real-life Example: The WannaCry ransomware attack in 2017 exploited a Windows vulnerability, infecting over 200,000 computers globally and demanding ransom payments for decryption keys.

2.4. Denial of Service (DoS) and Distributed Denial of Service (DDoS):

Description: actively disrupt services by overwhelming a system with traffic.

Nature: Active

Methods of Protection:

- DDoS Mitigation Services: employ services can identify and mitigate DDoS attacks.

- Load Balancing: distribute network traffic to prevent overload on specific servers.

- Real-life Example: The 2016 Dyn DDoS attack disrupted major websites and services by targeting the Domain Name System (DNS) provider Dyn, rendering many websites temporarily inaccessible.

2.5. Man-in-the-Middle (MitM) Attack:

Description: actively intercepts and potentially alters communication between two parties.

Nature: Active

Methods of Protection:

- Encryption: Use end-to-end encryption to secure communication.

- Secure Wi-Fi: Avoid public Wi-Fi for sensitive transactions.

- Real-life Example: In the 2013 Target data breach, attackers used a MitM attack to intercept and steal payment card data during transactions at Target stores.

2.6. SQL Injection:

Description: actively exploit vulnerabilities in database-backed applications by injecting malicious SQL code or Structured Query

Language, is a domain-specific programming language designed for managing and manipulating relational databases.

Nature: Active

Methods of Protection:

- Input Validation: implement input validation to sanitize user input.

- Parametrised Queries: use parametrised queries to prevent SQL injection.

- Real-life Example: The 2017 Equifax data breach involved attackers exploiting an SQL injection vulnerability to gain unauthorized access and steal sensitive personal information from millions of individuals.

2.7. Zero-Day Exploit:

Description: actively targets software vulnerabilities unknown to the software vendor.

Nature: Active

Methods of Protection:
- Regular Software Updates: keep software up to date to patch known vulnerabilities.

- Intrusion Detection Systems (IDS): use IDS to detect suspicious activities.

- Real-life Example: Stuxnet, discovered in 2010, was a worm that exploited multiple zero-day vulnerabilities to target Iran's nuclear facilities, highlighting the use of advanced malware for geopolitical purposes.

2.8. Cross-Site Scripting (XSS):

Description: actively injects malicious scripts into web pages viewed by other users.

Nature: Active

Methods of Protection:

- Input Validation: validate and sanitize user input on web applications.

- Content Security Policy (CSP): implement policies to control script execution.

- Real-life Example: The 2013 Adobe breach involved attackers exploiting an XSS vulnerability to compromise user accounts and expose sensitive information.

2.9.   Supply Chain Attacks:

Description: actively targets vulnerabilities in the supply chain to compromise third-party software or services.

Nature: Active

Methods of Protection:

- Vendor Security Assessment: assess and ensure the security practices of third-party vendors.

- Continuous Monitoring: monitor supply chain components for potential threats.

- Real-life Example: The SolarWinds cyberattack in 2020 involved compromising the software supply chain, leading to the distribution of malware that affected multiple organizations, including government agencies.

2.10.   Brute Force Attacks:

Description: actively attempts to gain unauthorized access by systematically trying all combinations of passwords or keys.

Nature: Active

Methods of Protection:

- Account Lockout Policies: implement policies to lock out accounts after multiple failed login attempts.

- Strong Password Policies: enforce the use of strong, complex passwords.

- Real-life Example: Credential stuffing attacks are common, with leaked username and password combinations from one breach being used to gain unauthorized access to other accounts.

Understanding whether a threat is passive or active helps cybersecurity professionals tailor their defense strategies. Both types require vigilant monitoring and proactive measures to mitigate the potential risks they pose.

V. LET'S EXAMINE THE PASSIVE THREATS

As the digital realm continues to advance, the threats that lurk in its shadows. Passive cyberattacks, particularly eavesdropping and monitoring, stand out as silent adversaries capable of wreaking havoc on digital ecosystems. This in-depth exploration will delve into the intricate workings of eavesdropping and monitoring, unraveling their implementation methods, dissecting the far-reaching consequences, and proposing comprehensive strategies to prevent and protect against these clandestine activities.

Implementation of Eavesdropping and Monitoring

1. Packet Sniffing and Data Interception

Eavesdropping often relies on exploiting vulnerabilities in communication protocols. Packet sniffing, a technique where attackers intercept and log data traveling over a network, provides an insider's view into the communication stream. This section will elaborate on how cybercriminals leverage packet sniffers to capture sensitive information and discuss the challenges in detecting such covert activities.

Packet sniffers, also known as network sniffers or protocol analyzers, are tools used to capture and analyze data packets transmitted over a network. While they have legitimate uses in network troubleshooting and analysis, cybercriminals can exploit them for malicious purposes. Here's an elaboration on how cybercriminals leverage packet sniffers and the challenges in detecting such covert activities:

1.1. Data Interception:

- Man-in-the-Middle Attacks: Cybercriminals can position themselves between the communication flow, intercepting and capturing data passing between two parties. Packet sniffers enable them to capture sensitive information, such as login credentials, financial details, or personal data.

1.2. Passive Eavesdropping:

- Monitoring Unencrypted Traffic: If network traffic is not encrypted, packet sniffers can easily capture and interpret the transmitted data. This is problematic on open Wi-Fi networks, where unencrypted data is more susceptible to interception.

1.3. Exploiting Weak Protocols:

- Protocol Vulnerabilities: Cybercriminals may exploit vulnerabilities in network protocols to gain unauthorized access to sensitive information. Packet sniffers help them identify weaknesses and collect data without raising suspicion.

1.4. Challenges in Detecting Covert Activities:

- Encryption Bypass: When using encrypted communication, it becomes challenging to decipher the intercepted data. Cybercriminals may employ additional techniques to bypass encryption or focus on capturing unencrypted data points.

- Stealthy Operation: Packet sniffers can operate silently, making it difficult for traditional security measures to detect their presence. Advanced attackers may use techniques like steganography to hide the sniffing activities within seemingly harmless network traffic.

- Legitimate Use Concerns: Distinguishing between legitimate and malicious use of packet sniffers can be challenging. System administrators and security teams often use similar tools for network troubleshooting, making it harder to identify malicious activities.

- Constantly Growing Tactics: Cybercriminals continually adapt their techniques to bypass detection mechanisms. As security technologies improve, attackers develop more sophisticated methods, making it an ongoing challenge for defenders to keep up.

- Encrypted Tunnels and VPNs: Cybercriminals may use encrypted tunnels or virtual private networks (VPNs) to further conceal their activities. This adds another layer of complexity in detecting and mitigating malicious packet sniffing.

In conclusion, the use of packet sniffers by cybercriminals poses a significant threat to the security of sensitive information. Detecting such covert activities requires a combination of advanced threat detection tools, encryption protocols, and constant vigilance to stay ahead of growing attack techniques.

2. Man-in-the-Middle (MitM) Attacks

MitM attacks present a sophisticated method for eavesdropping and positioning threat actors between communicating parties. By intercepting and altering data exchanges without detection, attackers gain access to confidential conversations, login credentials, and the ability to inject malicious content. This subsection will explore MitM attack scenarios, highlighting their potential impact on both individuals and organizations.

Man-in-the-Middle (MitM) attacks involve an attacker intercepting and potentially altering communication between two parties without their knowledge. These attacks can have severe consequences for both individuals and organizations. Here are some MitM attack scenarios and their potential affects:

2.1. Eavesdropping on Unsecured Wi-Fi Networks:

- Scenario: An attacker sets up an open Wi-Fi network or exploits vulnerabilities in an existing one.

- Impact on Individuals: Capturing sensitive information (login credentials, personal data) from individuals using the compromised network.

- Impact on Organizations: Employee credentials, company emails, and other sensitive information most likely will be intercepted, leading to unauthorized access to corporate networks.

2.2. DNS Spoofing:

- Scenario: Manipulating Domain Name System (DNS) responses to redirect users to malicious websites.

- Impact on Individuals: Users may unknowingly visit phishing sites, leading to the theft of login credentials or financial information.

- Impact on Organizations: Corporate users might be redirected to fake login pages, risking exposure of corporate credentials and sensitive information.

2.3. SSL Stripping:

- Scenario: Forcing a downgrade from secure HTTPS to unsecured HTTP, allowing the attacker to intercept and change data.

- Impact on Individuals: Sensitive information, such as login credentials and financial details, that can be intercepted.

- Impact on Organizations: Corporate users accessing sensitive company systems may unknowingly transmit unencrypted data, exposing it to interception.

2.4. Email Hijacking:

- Scenario: Intercepting emails between parties and potentially altering their content.

- Impact on Individuals: Unauthorized access to personal and sensitive emails, leading to privacy breaches.

- Impact on Organizations: Business emails can be intercepted, modified, or redirected, leading to potential fraud, data leakage, or disruption of communication.

2.5. Wi-Fi Pineapple* Attacks:

- Scenario: Using a device like the Wi-Fi Pineapple to trick devices into connecting, enabling the attacker to intercept traffic.

- Impact on Individuals: All communications in connected devices may be intercepted, including login credentials and personal data.

- Impact on Organizations: Employees connecting to compromised Wi-Fi networks may inadvertently expose corporate credentials and data.

* A Wi-Fi Pineapple is a small device used by cybersecurity experts to test the security of Wi-Fi networks. Unfortunately, could be misused for malicious purposes if not used properly.

2.6. Session Hijacking:

- Scenario: Stealing session tokens or cookies to impersonate a user and gain unauthorized access.

- Impact on Individuals: Unauthorized access to personal accounts, leading to identity theft or financial loss.

- Impact on Organizations: Attackers can gain access to sensitive corporate accounts and data, potentially leading to data breaches.

MitM attacks emphasize the importance of implementing robust security measures, such as encryption protocols, secure Wi-Fi practices, and user awareness training. Organizations and individuals need to be vigilant to protect against the potential impacts of these sophisticated attacks.

3. Silent Observation and Intelligent Monitoring

Monitoring activities involve the strategic observation of digital behaviors without direct interference. Advanced tools enable cybercriminals to track user behaviors, analyze network traffic patterns, and mine system logs for exploitable information.

This segment will review the nuances of silent observation, shedding light on the intelligent monitoring techniques that the threat actors employ to gather valuable intelligence over an extended period. Silent observation, also known as covert surveillance, refers to the subtle and undetected monitoring of individuals, organizations, or systems over an extended period. Threat actors use intelligent techniques to gather valuable intelligence without alerting their targets.

Here are some nuances of silent observation and the techniques employed by threat actors:

3.1. Passive Listening:

- Description: Threat actors engage in passive listening, intercepting, and analyzing communication without actively taking part.

- Techniques: Monitoring network traffic, eavesdropping on unsecured communications, or analyzing publicly available information without direct interaction.

3.2. Pattern Recognition:

- Description: Threat actors observe patterns in behavior, communication, or activities to extract meaningful intelligence.

- Techniques: Analyzing the timing and frequency of communications, identifying routines, and recognizing habits to predict future actions or events.

3.3. Social Engineering:

- Description: Manipulating individuals into divulging sensitive information through psychological tactics.

- Techniques: Phishing, pretexting, or impersonation to gain trust and access valuable information. This involves exploiting human vulnerabilities rather than technical weaknesses.

3.4. IoT Exploitation:

- Description: Leveraging vulnerabilities in Internet of Things (IoT) devices for silent observation. It refers to the network of physical objects or "things" embedded with sensors, software, and other technologies that enable them to connect and exchange data with other devices and systems over the internet.

- Techniques: Compromising smart devices, such as surveillance cameras, smart home gadgets, or industrial IoT sensors, to collect information without raising suspicion.

3.5. Steganography:

- Description: Concealing information within seemingly innocuous data to avoid detection.

- Techniques: Embedding intelligence within images, documents, or other files, making it difficult to discern hidden data during routine inspections.

3.6. Temporal and Spatial Analysis:

- Description: Analyzing data in relation to time and location to uncover patterns and trends.

- Techniques: Correlating data points over time or mapping the physical locations of individuals or assets to identify relationships, routines, or vulnerabilities.

3.7. Low and Slow Attacks:

- Description: Conducting attacks with minimal impact to avoid detection.

- Techniques: Gradual and subtle exploitation of vulnerabilities over an extended period, ensuring that security systems may not immediately recognize the ongoing threat.

3.8. Insider Threats:

- Description: Exploiting individuals with privileged access to gain intelligence from within an organization.

- Techniques: Co-opting employees or insiders to leak sensitive information, making it challenging to trace the source of the leak.

3.9. Unconventional Communication Channels:

- Description: Using non-traditional channels to exchange information.

- Techniques: Leveraging seemingly harmless platforms or channels that are not closely monitored for communication, making it difficult for security measures to detect malicious activity.

3.10. Custom Malware and Exploits:

- Description: Developing tailored malware or exploits for specific targets.

- Techniques: Crafting sophisticated malware that operates quietly and avoids detection by traditional security solutions, allowing threat actors to gather intelligence undetected.

In conclusion, silent observation requires a combination of technical prowess, social engineering skills, and a deep understanding of the target's environment.

Defending against such intelligent monitoring techniques involves a holistic approach, including advanced threat detection, employee awareness training, and regular security assessments.

Here are some examples of Passive Cyber Attacks - Eavesdropping and Monitoring

Stuxnet Worm (2010):

Type: Monitoring

Description: Stuxnet, a highly sophisticated computer worm discovered in 2010, was designed to target supervisory control and data acquisition (SCADA) systems. It specifically aimed at Iran's nuclear program, monitoring and altering the functionality of industrial processes. The creators of Stuxnet showed the ability to weaponized monitoring attacks in order to manipulate physical systems, emphasizing the potential ramifications of intelligence-gathering operations.

Equifax Data Breach (2017):

Type: Eavesdropping

Description: In one of the most significant data breaches in history, the Equifax breach of 2017 exposed the personal information of nearly 147 million individuals. The attackers exploited a vulnerability in Equifax's website software, allowing them to eavesdrop on sensitive data such as names, Social Security numbers, and credit card information. This event underscored the real-world impact of eavesdropping on a massive scale.

PRISM Surveillance Program (2013):

Type: Monitoring

Description: The PRISM program, operated by the U.S. National Security Agency (NSA), came to light in 2013 through the disclosures by Edward Snowden. PRISM involves the monitoring of communication data from major technology companies, including Microsoft, Google, and Apple. This revelation exposed a large-scale government monitoring effort, showcasing how intelligence agencies could leverage technology companies to conduct widespread surveillance.

Wi-Fi Eavesdropping - Google Street View (2010):

Type: Eavesdropping

Description: Google Street View cars inadvertently collected data from unsecured Wi-Fi networks as they roamed streets capturing images. This incident, discovered in 2010, revealed that Google had been unintentionally eavesdropping on unencrypted Wi-Fi communications, collecting sensitive information such as emails and passwords. The case highlighted the risks associated with unintentional eavesdropping in widespread data collection efforts.

Shadow Brokers Leak (2017):

Type: Monitoring

Description: The Shadow Brokers, a hacking group, gained notoriety in 2017 by leaking a series of sophisticated cyber tools allegedly developed by the NSA. These tools, including monitoring and eavesdropping capabilities, were later used in various cyberattacks, such as the WannaCry ransomware outbreak. The incident exposed how monitoring tools developed by intelligence agencies could be repurposed by malicious actors, leading to widespread cyber threats.

These real-world examples underscore the diverse nature of eavesdropping and monitoring attacks, ranging from state-sponsored surveillance to unintentional data collection.

They serve as cautionary tales, emphasizing the need for robust cybersecurity measures to mitigate the risks posed by these passive cyber threats.

4. Consequences of Passive Cyber Attacks

4.1. Identity Theft and Financial Fraud.

The consequences of eavesdropping and monitoring are far-reaching, with stolen personal data leading to identity theft and financial fraud.

This section will delve into real-world cases, examining how compromised login credentials, credit card information, and medical records can be monetized on the dark web.

The dark web is a portion of the internet that is intentionally hidden and is frequently associated with illegal activities. Criminals on the dark web monetize various types of stolen data, including compromised login credentials, credit card information, and medical records.

Here are real-world cases illustrating how these types of stolen data are exploited for financial gain:

- Compromised Login Credentials:

Case Example: Credential Stuffing Attacks

Monetization: Criminals use automated tools to test extensive sets of username-password combinations (obtained from data breaches) on various websites. Successful logins provide access to user accounts, which can be exploited for various purposes.

Profit Model: Stolen accounts are often sold on dark web marketplaces, forums, or private channels. Buyers may use these accounts for identity theft, unauthorized access to services, or further exploitation.

- Credit Card Information:

Case Example: Magecart Attacks

Monetization: Magecart attacks involve compromising e-commerce websites to steal credit card details entered by users during online transactions. These attacks often go undetected by website owners.

Profit Model: Stolen credit card information is sold on the dark web, where buyers may use it for fraudulent purchases, card cloning, or selling it further to other criminals. Some criminals also offer cash out services, where they convert stolen card data into physical items or cash.

- Medical Records:

Case Example: Community Health Systems (CHS) Data Breach

Monetization: In the CHS data breach, hackers gained access to many medical records. Medical records contain sensitive information such as patient names, addresses, Social Security numbers, and medical histories.

Profit Model: Stolen medical records can be sold on the dark web for identity theft, insurance fraud, or blackmail. Criminals may fraudulently use the information to get medical services, prescription drugs, or even commit more severe crimes.

- Ransomware Attacks:

Case Example: WannaCry Ransomware

Monetization: Ransomware encrypts files on victims' computers, rendering them inaccessible. In exchange for providing the decryption key, the attackers demand a ransom payment (often in cryptocurrency).

Profit Model: Victims who pay the ransom contribute to the financial success of the attackers. The dark web serves as a platform for ransomware operators to communicate with victims and receive payments anonymously.

- Personal Information:

Case Example: Equifax Data Breach

Monetization: The Equifax breach exposed personal information, including Social Security numbers and birthdates, of millions of individuals.

Profit Model: Criminals can use this information for identity theft, applying for credit in the victims' names, or selling the data on the dark web. The stolen information may also be used to craft more convincing phishing attacks.

In the above cases, the dark web acts as a marketplace where stolen data is traded and exploited for various criminal purposes. It highlights the importance of cybersecurity measures, such as robust authentication systems, encryption, and data protection practices, to mitigate the risks associated with data breaches and unauthorized access.

4.2. Corporate Espionage and Trade Secret Compromise.

In a corporate context, monitoring activities can cause significant financial losses and the compromise of trade secrets. Through real-world examples, this subsection will illustrate the potential damage to a company's competitive edge and reputation, emphasizing the importance of safeguarding intellectual property.

Safeguarding intellectual property (IP) is crucial for maintaining a company's competitive edge and reputation. Real-world examples show the potential damage that can occur when intellectual property is compromised. Here are some cases that highlight the impact on companies' competitiveness and reputation:

- Stuxnet Attack (2010):

Background: Stuxnet was a sophisticated computer worm designed to target supervisory control and data acquisition (SCADA) systems, particularly those used in Iran's nuclear program.

Impact on Competitiveness: The development and deployment of Stuxnet required significant resources and expertise. It is believed to have set back Iran's nuclear program and showed the potential for cyber-attacks on critical infrastructure.

Reputation Damage: While the Stuxnet attack was a covert state-sponsored operation, the incident raised concerns about the use of cyber weapons, leading to increased scrutiny of nation-state activities in cyberspace.

- SolarWinds Cyberattack (2020):

Background: The SolarWinds breach involved the insertion of a malicious code into the software supply chain, compromising many organizations, including government agencies and major corporations.

Impact on Competitiveness: The attackers gained access to sensitive information and intellectual property from various organizations. This might provide a competitive advantage to other entities or nations.

Reputation Damage: The incident led to a loss of trust in the affected companies and raised questions about the security of software supply chains. It highlighted the need for robust cybersecurity measures in the software development and distribution process.

- Uber Data Breach (2016):

Background: Uber experienced a data breach where hackers gained access to the personal information of 57 million users and drivers. Uber paid the hackers to keep the breach secret.

Impact on Competitiveness: The stolen data included personal information and driver's license details. Competitors might exploit this information to gain insights into Uber's user base and driver network.

Reputation Damage: Uber faced significant backlash for concealing the breach and paying the hackers. The incident damaged the company's reputation for transparency and data protection.

- Apple vs. Samsung Patent Wars:

Background: Apple and Samsung engaged in a series of high-profile patent infringement lawsuits related to smartphone design and features.

Impact on Competitiveness: Legal battles over intellectual property can cause financial losses and impact a company's ability to innovate without legal constraints.

Reputation Damage: The prolonged legal disputes between Apple and Samsung garnered significant public attention. While it didn't necessarily damage the companies' overall reputations, it highlighted the competitive intensity in the tech industry and the importance of protecting intellectual property.

- Chinese Economic Espionage (Various Incidents):

Background: many instances of economic espionage, where Chinese hackers targeted Western companies to steal intellectual property and trade secrets.

Impact on Competitiveness: Stolen intellectual property could give Chinese companies a competitive advantage by reducing research and development costs.

Reputation Damage: The persistent reports of Chinese cyber-espionage have contributed to strained international relations and distrust between companies and the Chinese government. This has led to concerns about engaging in business partnerships with Chinese entities.

The above real-world examples underscore the importance of safeguarding intellectual property not only for maintaining a competitive edge but also for preserving a company's reputation and trustworthiness in the eyes of customers, partners, and the public. Strong cybersecurity measures and ethical business practices are essential to mitigate the risks associated with IP theft and breaches.

4.3. The Stealthy Nature of Passive Attacks.

The insidious nature of passive cyberattacks means that victims often remain unaware until substantial damage has been done. This segment will explore the challenges organizations face in detecting eavesdropping and monitoring activities promptly, complicating incident response efforts.

Detecting eavesdropping and monitoring activities promptly poses significant challenges for organizations, complicating incident response efforts. Eavesdropping refers to the unauthorized interception of communication, and monitoring activities may involve covert surveillance. Here are the challenges organizations face in identifying such activities in a timely manner:

- Passive Nature of Eavesdropping:

Challenge: Eavesdropping is often a passive activity where attackers quietly intercept and analyze communications without actively altering data. This makes it difficult for organizations to detect anomalies or suspicious behavior that may show eavesdropping.

- Encryption Bypass:

Challenge: Advanced eavesdroppers may employ techniques to bypass encryption mechanisms. If communications are encrypted, traditional monitoring solutions may not effectively detect unauthorized interception, as the data appears secure and unaltered.

- Steganography and Covert Channels:

Challenge: Eavesdroppers may use steganography to hide their activities within seemingly innocuous data or employ covert communication channels that are difficult to detect. Traditional security measures may not recognize such hidden communication methods.

- Insider Threats:

Challenge: Eavesdropping activities may involve insiders who have legitimate access to the network or sensitive information. Detecting malicious intent among employees or contractors can be challenging, especially if the eavesdropping is done subtly over an extended period.

- Slow and Low Tactics:

Challenge: Eavesdropping attacks often employ "slow and low" tactics, meaning the attackers gradually collect information over an extended period to avoid detection. This slow pace can make it challenging to identify patterns or anomalies that would trigger alerts.

- Legitimate Monitoring Tools:

Challenge: Organizations often use legitimate monitoring tools for network performance and security. Distinguishing between allowed and unauthorized monitoring can be difficult, especially if the eavesdropper leverages tools that blend in with standard network management practices.

- Evasion Techniques:

Challenge: Sophisticated eavesdroppers use evasion techniques to avoid detection by traditional security solutions. This may include manipulating network traffic patterns, disguising their presence, or exploiting vulnerabilities in monitoring systems.

- Diverse Attack Vectors:

Challenge: Eavesdropping activities can occur through various attack vectors, including compromised hardware, software vulnerabilities, or physical access to network infrastructure. Organizations need to monitor and secure a diverse range of entry points, making detection more complex.

- Global and Remote Operations:

Challenge: Eavesdroppers may operate from different geographic locations, making it challenging for organizations to identify and attribute the source of the activities. Remote operations can further complicate incident response efforts.

- Lack of Behavioral Baselines:

Challenge: Establishing accurate behavioral baselines for normal network and user activities is crucial for detecting anomalies. However, defining these baselines can be challenging, especially in dynamic and growing network environments.

To address these challenges, organizations need advanced threat detection solutions, continuous monitoring, and active security measures. Developing a comprehensive incident response plan that includes regular security assessments, employee training, and collaboration with threat intelligence sources is essential for mitigating the risks associated with eavesdropping and covert monitoring activities.

5. Prevention and Protection Strategies

Encryption Protocols and Data-in-Transit Security.

To counter passive cyberattacks, organizations must implement robust encryption protocols. This subsection will provide a detailed analysis of Transport Layer Security (TLS) for web traffic and Virtual Private Networks (VPNs) for securing remote communications.

5.1. Transport Layer Security (TLS) for Web Traffic:

Overview:

Purpose: TLS is a cryptographic protocol designed to secure communication over a computer network, especially on the internet. It protects the privacy and integrity of data between communicating applications.

Encryption: TLS uses encryption algorithms to protect data in transit. It secures web traffic by encrypting information exchanged between a user's browser and a web server, preventing eavesdropping and tampering.

Key Features:

Encryption Algorithms: TLS supports various encryption algorithms, including symmetric and asymmetric cryptography. Common algorithms include AES for symmetric encryption and RSA for key exchange.

Certificate-based Authentication: TLS uses digital certificates to authenticate the identity of servers and, optionally, clients. This helps ensure users are connecting to legitimate websites and not falling victim to man-in-the-middle attacks.

Handshake Process:

Key Exchange: During the TLS handshake, the client and server agree on encryption parameters, exchange cryptographic keys, and verify each other's digital certificates.

Perfect Forward Secrecy (PFS): Many TLS implementations support PFS, ensuring that even if a long-term key is compromised, past communications remain secure.

Versions:

Evolution: TLS has undergone multiple versions, with TLS 1.3 being the latest (as of my last knowledge update in January 2022). Newer versions address vulnerabilities, improve security, and enhance performance.

Challenges and Considerations:

Legacy Support: Compatibility with older protocols can be a challenge. However, it's crucial to prioritize security over compatibility and encourage the adoption of the latest TLS versions.

Configuration Management: Proper TLS configuration is essential. Misconfigurations, weak ciphers, or outdated protocols can introduce vulnerabilities.

5.2. Virtual Private Networks (VPNs) for Securing Remote Communications:

Overview:

Purpose: VPNs establish secure, encrypted connections over the internet, enabling users to access a private network from remote locations. They enhance privacy and security for remote communications.

Types: VPNs can be categorized into various types, including site-to-site, remote access, and peer-to-peer VPNs.

Key Features:

Tunneling Protocols: VPNs use tunneling protocols to encapsulate and encrypt data for secure transmission. IPsec, SSL/TLS, and PPTP are examples of common protocols.

Authentication and Authorization: Users and devices connecting to a VPN are authenticated before gaining access. Authorization policies define the level of access granted based on user credentials.

Types of VPNs:

Site-to-Site VPNs: Connect entire networks securely over the internet, commonly used for connecting branch offices.

Remote Access VPNs: Enable individual users to connect to a private network from remote locations, providing secure access to resources.

SSL/TLS VPNs: Use the SSL/TLS protocols for secure remote access. They are often web-based and do not require dedicated client software.

Security Considerations:

End-to-End Encryption: VPNs provide end-to-end encryption, securing data from the user's device to the VPN server and, if configured properly, to the destination server.

Logging Policies: VPN providers should have clear logging policies to protect user privacy. Some VPN services claim to have a "no-logs" policy, meaning they do not collect or store user data.

Challenges and Considerations:

VPN Client Security: The security of the user's device, especially the VPN client, is crucial. Vulnerabilities in the client software can be exploited to compromise the security of the VPN connection.

Detection and Prevention of VPN Tunneling: Some organizations may face challenges in detecting and preventing unauthorized VPN use, especially if it is against company policy.

5.3. Future Trends:

Zero-Trust Architecture: VPNs are growing within the context of zero-trust security models. Continuous verification and monitoring of users and devices, even within the VPN, are becoming more important.

Secure Access Service Edge (SASE): The integration of security services with wide-area networking is a trend, combining elements of SD-WAN and security services to provide a more comprehensive solution.

In summary, both TLS for web traffic and VPNs for remote communications play crucial roles in securing data and communication over the internet. They provide encryption, authentication, and privacy features essential for protecting sensitive information in an increasingly connected and remote work-oriented digital landscape.

5.4. Regular Software Updates and Vulnerability Patching.

Regularly updating and patching software and systems is critical to closing potential vulnerabilities that attackers might exploit for eavesdropping or monitoring. This segment will explore the challenges of maintaining an updated infrastructure and propose guidelines for effective vulnerability management.

5.5. Challenges of Maintaining an Updated Infrastructure:

- Complexity of IT Environments:

Challenge: Modern IT infrastructures are often complex, comprising various technologies, platforms, and interconnected systems. Updating such diverse environments can be challenging and may lead to compatibility issues.

- Legacy Systems and Software:

Challenge: Organizations often rely on legacy systems and software that may not receive regular updates or support. Integrating these systems with newer technologies poses challenges in maintaining a secure and updated environment.

- Interdependencies and Integration Issues:

Challenge: Interdependencies between different components of the infrastructure can complicate updates. A change in one system may affect others, potentially leading to downtime or functionality issues.

- Resource Restrictions:

Challenge: Limited resources, including time, budget, and human resources, can hinder the ability to keep infrastructure components up to date. Organizations may struggle to allocate sufficient resources for regular updates.

- Vendor Patching Timelines:

Challenge: Organizations rely on vendors to release patches and updates for the software and systems they use. Delays in vendor patching timelines can leave systems vulnerable, especially if a critical vulnerability is exploited before a patch is available.

- Regulatory Compliance:

Challenge: Compliance requirements often mandate that organizations maintain secure and up-to-date systems. Meeting these compliance standards while managing other aspects of the infrastructure can be demanding.

- User Resistance to Changes:

Challenge: Users may resist changes to interfaces or functionalities introduced with updates. Resistance can lead to delays in implementing necessary security patches and updates.

- Testing and Validation:

Challenge: Before deploying updates, thorough testing and validation are essential to ensure that the updates do not introduce additional issues or disrupt existing workflows. Testing can be time-consuming and resource intensive.

6. Guidelines for Effective Vulnerability Management:

6.1. Asset Inventory and Prioritization:

- Maintain an up-to-date inventory of all assets in the infrastructure. Prioritize assets based on their criticality to business operations, focusing on the most critical systems first.

6.2. Regular Vulnerability Assessments:

- Conduct regular vulnerability assessments to identify weaknesses in the infrastructure. Automated tools and manual testing can help uncover vulnerabilities that need immediate attention.

6.3. Patch Management:

- Implement a robust patch management process. Regularly review and apply security patches provided by vendors promptly. Patch management tools that are automated can help to speed up the process.

6.4. Continuous Monitoring:

- Implement continuous monitoring solutions to detect vulnerabilities and potential security threats in real-time. This allows for immediate response to emerging security issues.

6.5. Change Management:

- Implement a formal change management process to handle updates and changes systematically. This includes testing, validation, and communication with stakeholders to minimize disruptions.

6.6. Education and Awareness:

- Educate employees and users about the importance of updates and their role in maintaining a secure environment. Create awareness about the potential risks associated with unpatched systems.

6.7. Automation and Orchestration:

- Use automation and orchestration tools to streamline the update process. Automation can help schedule updates during non-business hours and reduce the manual effort required.

6.8. Incident Response Plan:

- Develop and regularly update an incident response plan that includes procedures for handling vulnerabilities and security incidents. This ensures a swift and coordinated response to security threats.

6.9. Vendor Relationship Management:

- Establish strong relationships with vendors and stay informed about their security practices. Engage in active communication to receive timely information about patches and updates.

6.10. Regular Training and Drills:

- Conduct regular training sessions and drills to ensure that the IT team is well-prepared to handle updates and respond to security incidents. This includes practicing incident response procedures.

By adopting these guidelines, organizations can enhance their vulnerability management processes, reduce the risk of security breaches, and maintain a more resilient and secure IT infrastructure. Regular monitoring, continuous improvement, and an active approach to security are key elements of effective vulnerability management.

7. Network Security Measures: Segmentation and Access Controls

Implementing robust network security measures, including network segmentation and access controls, can limit the impact of monitoring activities. This subsection will delve into the benefits of compartmentalizing sensitive data and restricting access to minimize the surface area available to attackers.

Compartmentalizing sensitive data and restricting access is a fundamental security practice that offers several benefits in minimizing the surface area available to attackers. This approach enhances the overall security posture of an organization and mitigates the impact of potential security incidents. Here are the key benefits of compartmentalization and access restriction:

7.1 Reduced Attack Surface:

Benefit: Compartmentalization limits the exposure of sensitive data to only specific allowed areas of the network. By segmenting the network and restricting access, the attack surface available to potential attackers is significantly reduced. This makes moving laterally within the network more difficult for attackers.

7.2. Mitigation of Lateral Movement:

Benefit: Compartmentalization inhibits lateral movement within the network. Even if an attacker gains access to one compartment, they are less likely to traverse to other compartments without proper authorization. This containment prevents the spread of attacks and limits the potential damage.

7.3. Isolation of High-Value Assets:

Benefit: High-value assets, such as sensitive databases or critical systems, can be isolated in dedicated compartments. This ensures that even if one compartment is compromised, the most critical assets remain protected, minimizing the impact of a security breach.

7.4. Granular Access Control:

Benefit: By compartmentalizing data, organizations can implement granular access controls. This means that only individuals or systems with specific authorization can access certain compartments. Fine-grained access control enhances security by limiting exposure to a need-to-know basis.

7.5. Enhanced Data Privacy and Compliance:

Benefit: Compartmentalization supports compliance with data privacy regulations. It helps organizations show a firm commitment to protecting sensitive information by implementing measures to minimize unauthorized access and maintain data confidentiality.

7.6. Containment of Security Incidents:

Benefit: In the event of a security incident, compartmentalization helps contain the impact. Isolating affected compartments prevents the spread of malware, limits data exposure, and allows for more effective incident response and remediation efforts.

7.7. Facilitation of Least Privilege Principle:

Benefit: Compartmentalization aligns with the least privilege principle, ensuring that users and systems have only the minimum level of access necessary to perform their duties. This principle reduces the risk of unintended access and potential misuse of sensitive data.

7.8. Defense-in-Depth Strategy:

Benefit: Compartmentalization is an integral part of a defense-in-depth strategy, where multiple layers of security measures are implemented. By layering security controls, organizations create a more resilient defense against various attack vectors, making it harder for attackers to exploit vulnerabilities.

7.9. Improved Incident Detection:

Benefit: Compartmentalization facilitates better monitoring and detection of security incidents. Unusual activities or unauthorized access attempts within a compartment can be detected more easily, allowing for prompt investigation and response.

7.10. Adaptability to Dynamic Threat Landscape:

Benefit: As the threat landscape grows, compartmentalization provides a flexible and adaptive security framework. Organizations can adjust compartmentalization strategies to address new threats, emerging vulnerabilities, or changes in business requirements.

In conclusion, compartmentalizing sensitive data and restricting access is an active and effective security measure that strengthens an organization's resilience against cyber threats. This approach not only limits the attack surface but also promotes a security architecture that aligns with guidelines and regulatory requirements.

8. User Education and Awareness Programs

User education and awareness play a pivotal role in preventing passive cyberattacks. This section will explore the dynamics of social engineering and highlight the importance of empowering individuals to recognize and resist these tactics, reducing the likelihood of falling victim to eavesdropping-enabled attacks.

8.1. Dynamics of Social Engineering:

Social engineering is a manipulation that exploits human psychology to deceive individuals into divulging confidential information, performing actions, or compromising security.

Often involves exploiting trust, authority, urgency, or fear achieving the attacker's goals. Eavesdropping-enabled attacks may leverage information gathered through social engineering to target individuals or organizations.

Understanding the dynamics of social engineering is crucial for recognizing and resisting these tactics:

8.2. Pretexting:

- Dynamic: Attackers create a fabricated scenario or pretext to trick individuals into disclosing sensitive information. This could involve posing as a trusted entity, such as an IT support technician or a colleague, to gain access to confidential data.

8.3. Phishing:

- Dynamic: Phishing involves sending deceptive emails, messages, or websites that appear legitimate to trick individuals into revealing sensitive information, such as login credentials or financial details. Eavesdropping can enhance phishing attacks by tailoring them with specific knowledge about the target.

8.4. Baiting:

- Dynamic: Baiting involves enticing individuals with something attractive, like a free software download, to trick them into revealing sensitive information. Eavesdropping can help attackers customize baiting attempts based on the target's interests or preferences.

8.5. Quid Pro Quo:

- Dynamic: In quid pro quo attacks, attackers offer something in exchange for information, such as posing as a helpful service provider or offering technical support. Eavesdropping enables attackers to gather intelligence about the target's needs and preferences.

8.6. Impersonation:

- Dynamic: Attackers may impersonate authoritative figures, colleagues, or service providers to gain trust and deceive individuals into taking specific actions. Eavesdropping provides insights that make impersonation more convincing.

8.7. Tailgating and Piggybacking:

- Dynamic: information gathered through eavesdropping can facilitate physical security aspects like tailgating (following someone without authorization) or piggybacking (gaining unauthorized access by exploiting someone else's entry).

9. Importance of Empowering Individuals:

9.1. Awareness and Education:

- Importance: Educating individuals about social engineering tactics and the potential risks associated with eavesdropping is crucial. Increased awareness enables individuals to recognize red flags and be more vigilant.

9.2. Phishing Simulation Training:

- Importance: Conducting phishing simulation exercises helps individual's experience simulated social engineering attacks in a controlled environment. This hands-on approach enhances their ability to identify phishing attempts and respond appropriately.

9.3. Regular Security Training Programs:

- Importance: Implementing regular security training programs keeps individuals informed about the latest social engineering tactics. It empowers them to stay updated on security guidelines and be resilient against growing threats.

9.4. Encouraging a Culture of Suspicion:

- Importance: Fostering a culture where individuals are encouraged to verify requests, double-check unexpected communications, and question unusual scenarios helps create a more security-conscious environment.

9.5. Multi-Factor Authentication (MFA):

- Importance: Implementing MFA adds an extra layer of security, making it more difficult for attackers to gain unauthorized access even if credentials are compromised through social engineering attacks.

9.6. Clear Communication Channels for Reporting:

- Importance: Establishing clear and accessible channels for reporting suspicious activities or potential social engineering attempts encourages individuals to share concerns and facilitates prompt incident response.

9.7. Regular Security Updates and Reminders:

- Importance: Sending regular security updates and reminders reinforces key security principles. Reminders about the dangers of social engineering and the importance of safeguarding sensitive information can contribute to a security-conscious mindset.

9.8. Testing and Assessments:

- Importance: Conducting periodic security assessments, including simulated social engineering tests, helps organizations identify vulnerabilities and areas for improvement. This active approach strengthens defenses against social engineering attacks.

9.9. Technical Controls and Safeguards:

- Importance: Implementing technical controls, such as email filtering, endpoint protection, and network monitoring, helps detect and mitigate social engineering attacks. These controls act as additional layers of defense, complementing user awareness efforts.

By empowering individuals with knowledge, training, and the right mindset, organizations can significantly reduce the likelihood of falling victim to social engineering tactics, including those facilitated by eavesdropping. It transforms employees into a valuable line of defense against growing cyber threats.

9.10. Conclusion:

Safeguarding against passive cyberattacks demands a multifaceted approach that combines technological defenses, active measures, and user education. This comprehensive exploration has shed light on the intricacies of eavesdropping and monitoring, providing a roadmap for organizations to fortify their digital perimeters and minimize the risk of falling prey to these covert threats.

In the dynamic landscape of cybersecurity, the menace of active cyberattacks remains a persistent and growing threat. Unlike passive attacks that focus on information gathering, active cyberattacks involve direct and malicious actions to compromise the security and functionality of digital systems. This book aims to provide an in-depth exploration of what active cyberattacks entail, how they are applied, the potential damage they can inflict, and effective strategies to safeguard against them. Real-life examples will be provided to illustrate the severity and sophistication of these attacks.

VI. UNDERSTANDING ACTIVE CYBER ATTACKS

Active cyberattacks, also known as offensive cyber operations, involve intentional and malicious actions carried out by cyber adversaries with the goal of infiltrating, disrupting, or manipulating computer systems, networks, or digital infrastructure.

Unlike passive attacks, which focus on unauthorized access or eavesdropping, active cyberattacks involve direct engagement and manipulation of targeted systems.

Individuals, groups, or nation-states with various motives typically conduct these attacks, including espionage, financial gain, activism, or sabotage.

Here's a list of common active cyberattacks:

1. Malware Attacks: Delivery of malicious software, such as viruses, worms, trojans, and ransomware, to compromise systems or steal sensitive information.

- Viruses: Self-replicating programs that infect other files or systems.

- Worms: Self-replicating malware that spreads across networks without user intervention.

- Trojans: Malicious software disguised as legitimate to deceive users into executing them.

2. Phishing Attacks: Deceptive tactics, often using fraudulent emails, messages.

- Email Phishing: Deceptive emails aiming to trick recipients into revealing sensitive information or installing malware.

- Spear Phishing: Targeted phishing attacks tailored to specific individuals or organizations.

3. **Ransomware Attacks:** Encrypting files or systems and demanding a ransom for decryption.

4. **Distributed Denial-of-Service (DDoS):** Overwhelming a system or network with an excessive amount of traffic to render it inaccessible.

5. **Man-in-the-Middle (MitM):**

- Session Hijacking: Taking over an active session between two parties.

- SSL Stripping: Forcing a connection over HTTP instead of HTTPS to intercept data.

6. **SQL Injection:** Exploiting vulnerabilities in database software to execute malicious SQL statements.

7. **Cross-Site Scripting (XSS):** Injecting malicious scripts into web pages viewed by other users.

8. **Brute Force Attacks:** Repeatedly trying various combinations to guess passwords or encryption keys.

9. **Zero-Day Exploits:** Leveraging vulnerabilities unknown to software developers for which no patch or fix exists.

10. **Insider Threats:** Malicious actions by individuals within an organization to exploit vulnerabilities or leak sensitive information.

11. **IoT-Based Attacks:** Exploiting vulnerabilities in Internet of Things devices to gain access to networks or data.

12. **Supply Chain Attacks:** Compromising a product or service through its supply chain to reach the end user.

13. Fileless Attacks: Exploiting system vulnerabilities without leaving traditional traces like files or scripts.

VII. IMPLEMENTATION OF ACTIVE ATTACKS

1. Malware Infections: Active attacks frequently involve the deployment of malicious software, commonly known as malware. This can take various forms, including viruses, ransomware, trojans, and worms.

Malware exploits vulnerabilities in software or relies on deceptive tactics to infiltrate systems and execute malicious actions.

Example: The infamous WannaCry ransomware attack in 2017 exploited a vulnerability in Windows systems, spreading rapidly and encrypting data, demanding ransom payments for decryption keys.

2. Phishing and Social Engineering: Social engineering is a cornerstone of active cyberattacks, often taking the form of phishing campaigns.

Attackers craft deceptive emails or messages to manipulate individuals into divulging sensitive information, clicking on malicious links, or downloading malware.

Example: A spear-phishing attack targeting employees of a financial institution led to unauthorized access to sensitive customer data, resulting in financial losses and reputational damage.

3. Denial of Service (DoS) and Distributed Denial of Service (DDoS): Active attacks on availability involve overwhelming a target system, network, or service to disrupt normal operations.

DoS and DDoS attacks use various means, such as flooding the target with traffic or exploiting vulnerabilities to exhaust resources.

Example: The 2016 Dyn DDoS attack disrupted major internet services by targeting the Domain Name System (DNS), rendering several high-profile websites inaccessible.

VIII. POTENTIAL DAMAGE FROM ACTIVE ATTACKS

1. **Data Breaches:** Active attacks often lead to unauthorized access and exfiltration of sensitive data.

Data breaches can have severe consequences, including financial losses, regulatory penalties, and long-term damage to an organization's reputation.

2. **Financial Losses:** Ransomware attacks, a subset of active attacks, encrypt critical data and demand ransom payments. Failure to comply can cause permanent data loss, operational disruption, and financial ramifications.
    *   **Direct Financial Theft**: Active attacks can lead to direct theft of funds or valuable assets. For instance, techniques like phishing, social engineering, or malware can compromise bank accounts, cryptocurrency wallets, or online payment systems.
    *   **Business Disruption**: Disrupting critical systems or services through active attacks can result in significant financial losses due to downtime, reduced productivity, and missed business opportunities. This could occur through techniques like DDoS (Distributed Denial of Service) attacks targeting essential services or ransomware locking down systems until a ransom is paid.
    *   **Fraudulent Transactions**: Active attacks may involve manipulating financial systems to carry out fraudulent transactions, such as unauthorized wire transfers or altering payment details.

3. **Reputational Damage**:

- **Loss of Trust**: Breaches resulting from active attacks can erode trust between customers, partners, and stakeholders. Public disclosure of sensitive information or inability to protect customer data damages the reputation of organizations.
- **Brand Devaluation**: Organizations that fall victim to active attacks may suffer from a devaluation of their brand as customers, investors, and partners lose confidence in their ability to safeguard sensitive information.
- **Legal Consequences**: Negative publicity resulting from active attacks can lead to legal actions, fines, or regulatory penalties, further tarnishing the reputation of affected entities.

3. **Intellectual Property Theft**:
   - Active attacks targeting intellectual property (IP) can result in the theft or unauthorized access to proprietary information, trade secrets, or research and development data. Competitors or threat actors may exploit stolen IP for financial gain, competitive advantage, or to undermine the original organization's market position.

4. **Operational Disruption:**
   - Active attacks can disrupt essential services, leading to downtime, loss of productivity, and damage to an organization's ability to function effectively.

5. **Privacy Violations**:
   - Active attacks compromising sensitive personal data can lead to privacy violations, identity theft, or exposure to blackmail and extortion. Such breaches can have profound implications for individuals, including financial hardship, emotional distress, and damage to personal and professional relationships.

6. **National Security Risks**:
   - Active attacks targeting government agencies, military systems, or critical infrastructure pose significant national security risks. These attacks can disrupt essential services, compromise classified information, or even undermine the sovereignty of a nation.

7. **Human Safety Concerns**:

- In certain cases, active attacks on systems controlling transportation, healthcare, or emergency services can pose direct risks to human safety. For example, attacks on medical devices or transportation systems can lead to injuries or loss of life.

IX. PROTECTING AGAINST ACTIVE ATTACKS:

1. Regular Software Updates: Timely software updates are crucial in mitigating the risk of active attacks. Regular patches and updates help address known vulnerabilities, reducing the likelihood of exploitation.

2. Employee Training: Educating users about the dangers of phishing and social engineering is vital. Employees should be trained to recognize and report suspicious activities, reducing the risk of falling victim to deceptive tactics.

3. Network Security Measures: Implementing robust network security measures, including firewalls, intrusion detection systems, and access controls, can help detect and prevent unauthorized access.

Active cyberattacks have become a formidable and pervasive threat in today's interconnected world. As we've explored the intricacies of these malicious endeavors from targeted malware and data breaches to ransomware and supply chain compromises. The digital landscape is fraught with unseen adversaries seeking to exploit vulnerabilities for various purposes.

The potential damage wrought by active cyberattacks goes beyond the virtual realm, extending into the very fabric of our physical infrastructure, economic systems, and personal lives. The examples provided, including Stuxnet's impact on critical infrastructure and the widespread consequences of data breaches like Equifax, underscore the urgency for robust cybersecurity measures.

Faced with these growing threats, it is imperative for individuals, organizations, and governments to adopt an active stance. Cybersecurity is no longer a mere technological concern; it is a collective responsibility that demands continuous vigilance, adaptability, and resilience.

X. REAL-LIFE EXAMPLES

1. WannaCry Ransomware (2017):

The WannaCry ransomware attack in 2017 was a type of widespread cyberattack that specifically targeted Windows operating systems. It was classified as a ransomware attack because its primary goal was to encrypt files on infected computers and demand a ransom payment in cryptocurrency, (typically Bitcoin), from the victims in exchange for the decryption key.

Key characteristics of the WannaCry ransomware attack include:

Propagation Method: WannaCry used a vulnerability in Microsoft Windows known as EternalBlue, which was originally discovered by the U.S. National Security Agency (NSA) and later leaked by a hacking group called the Shadow Brokers. The ransomware spread rapidly by exploiting the EternalBlue vulnerability, enabling it to move laterally across connected systems within a network.

Encryption and Ransom Demand: Once a system was infected, WannaCry encrypted files on the victim's computer, rendering them inaccessible. The ransomware then displayed a ransom note, demanding payment in Bitcoin to decrypt the files. The victims were threatened with permanent data loss if the ransom was not paid within a specified time frame.

Worm-Like Behavior: One notable aspect of WannaCry was its ability to self-propagate like a worm. After infecting one system, it could automatically spread to other vulnerable systems without user interaction. The worm-like behavior contributed to the rapid and widespread nature of the attack, affecting organizations and individuals globally.

Impact and Targets: The WannaCry attack had a significant impact on a wide range of organizations, including healthcare institutions, government agencies, and businesses. Critical systems, such as those in the healthcare sector, were particularly affected, leading to disruptions in medical services.

Kill Switch Discovery: A cybersecurity researcher named Marcus Hutchins discovered a "kill switch" in the ransomware code. By registering a specific domain, the spread of WannaCry could be temporarily halted. The activation of the kill switch helped slow down the attack, but not before it had already affected many systems.

Attribution and Motivation: Attribution for the WannaCry attack was linked to the North Korea government, particularly the Lazarus Group, a state-sponsored hacking group associated with North Korea. The motivation behind the attack was believed to be both financial (ransom payments) and disruptive, potentially causing chaos and damage to the targeted systems.

The WannaCry ransomware attack highlighted the importance of promptly patching software vulnerabilities, maintaining up-to-date security practices, and being vigilant against emerging cyber threats. It also underscored the potential impact of ransomware on critical infrastructure and the need for global cooperation in addressing cybersecurity challenges.

2. NotPetya (2017):

Initially disguised as ransomware, NotPetya was later revealed to be a destructive wiper malware. It caused widespread damage, emphasizing the need for resilient data backup and recovery mechanisms. The NotPetya cyberattack in 2017 was a destructive and sophisticated malware campaign that targeted computers primarily in Ukraine.

However, it quickly spread globally, affecting organizations across various sectors. While initially believed to be a variant of the Petya ransomware, further analysis revealed that NotPetya had a different purpose and was more focused on causing disruption than financial gain.

The attack is often classified as a "wiper" rather than a traditional ransomware attack.

Here are key characteristics of the NotPetya attack:

Wiper Characteristics: Unlike typical ransomware, where the primary motive is to encrypt files and demand a ransom for decryption, NotPetya was designed to overwrite and destroy data on infected systems irreversibly. The attackers did not provide a workable way for victims to recover their data even if they paid a ransom, leading security experts to believe that the primary goal was disruption rather than financial gain.

Propagation Method: NotPetya used a compromised software update mechanism for a Ukrainian accounting software called M.E.Doc to spread across networks. The attackers compromised the update process, allowing them to deliver the malware to many organizations that used the M.E.Doc software.

EternalPetya and NSA Exploit: NotPetya leveraged the EternalBlue exploit, the same exploit used in the WannaCry ransomware attack. EternalBlue was part of a collection of hacking tools initially developed by the U.S. National Security Agency (NSA) and later leaked by a hacking group called the Shadow Brokers.

Global Impact: While the initial target seemed to be Ukraine, the NotPetya attack quickly spread globally, affecting organizations in various countries. Companies in sectors such as shipping, manufacturing, energy, and healthcare reported significant disruptions to their operations.

False Ransom Note: NotPetya displayed a ransom note demanding a Bitcoin payment for the alleged decryption key. However, analysis of the malware revealed it was not designed to provide a functional method for decrypting files. The false ransom notes further emphasized that the primary goal was not financial extortion.

Attribution Challenges: Attribution for the NotPetya attack has been a subject of debate among cybersecurity experts. While initial reports suggested a criminal group or state-sponsored actors, attributing the attack definitively has proven challenging. Some analysts believe that the intent of the attackers was to create chaos and disrupt operations rather than achieve specific geopolitical or financial objectives.

Post-Incident Analysis: NotPetya raised awareness about the potential impact of destructive malware attacks and highlighted the importance of securing software update mechanisms. The incident prompted organizations to reevaluate their cybersecurity practices, including patch management, network segmentation, and incident response capabilities.

In summary, the NotPetya attack was a highly destructive and disruptive cyber campaign that went beyond traditional ransomware tactics. It showcased the potential dangers of malware designed to cause widespread damage and underscored the importance of robust cybersecurity measures to prevent and mitigate such threats.

3. Stuxnet Worm (2010):

The Stuxnet worm, discovered in 2010, was a highly sophisticated and targeted cyber-weapon designed to sabotage Iran's nuclear program. Unlike typical malware or worms. Stuxnet was a complex and unprecedented cyber-espionage tool that specifically aimed to compromise and damage industrial systems, particularly those used in uranium enrichment facilities. The attack type associated with Stuxnet is often categorized as a "cyber-weapon" or a "cyber-physical attack" because of its unique characteristics.

Here are key aspects of the Stuxnet attack:

Attack Type: Targeted Malware

Description: Stuxnet was a sophisticated worm designed to target supervisory control and data acquisition (SCADA) systems. It specifically aimed at disrupting Iran's nuclear program by manipulating programmable logic controllers (PLCs). This marked a significant shift, as Stuxnet showed the potential for cyberattacks to cause physical damage to critical infrastructure.

Targeted Industrial Systems: Stuxnet targeted Supervisory Control and Data Acquisition (SCADA) systems and programmable logic controllers (PLCs), which are crucial components in industrial and critical infrastructure settings. The primary aim was to disrupt and damage Iran's uranium enrichment centrifuges by manipulating the control systems.

Zero-Day Exploits: Stuxnet employed multiple zero-day exploits, exploiting previously unknown vulnerabilities in software. This made it highly effective and difficult to detect or counter quickly. Using zero-day exploits highlighted the advanced and well-funded nature of the attack.

Propagation Methods: Stuxnet used various propagation methods, including exploiting Windows vulnerabilities, spreading through removable drives, and using a mechanism to propagate within air-gapped (physically isolated) networks. The worm showed a level of sophistication in its ability to move laterally across systems and networks.

Targeted Code Injection: Stuxnet employed a unique method of code injection into PLCs, causing the centrifuges to behave in a way that led to physical damage. The code injection involved changing the programmable logic of the industrial controllers to manipulate the speed and operation of the centrifuges without raising suspicion.

Dual Payloads: Stuxnet had two distinct payloads: one designed to target Siemens PLCs in industrial systems and another to mask its presence and thwart detection efforts. The dual payloads allowed the malware to operate covertly while carrying out its destructive objectives.

Specificity and Complexity: Stuxnet was highly specialized for its intended target, Iran's Natanz nuclear facility. It contained detailed knowledge of the specific control systems used in the facility. The complexity of Stuxnet suggested the involvement of a well-funded and technically advanced actor, leading to speculation about state-sponsored involvement.

Geopolitical Implications: Stuxnet is widely believed to be a state-sponsored cyber-weapon, with speculation pointing to the involvement of the United States and Israel. The attack marked a new era in cyber warfare, demonstrating the potential for targeted and destructive cyber-physical attacks on critical infrastructure.

Discovery and Attribution Challenges: Stuxnet initially went undetected for an extended period, highlighting the challenges of attributing cyberattacks to specific actors. Its discovery and subsequent analysis by cybersecurity researchers revealed the unprecedented nature of the cyber-weapon.

In summary, Stuxnet represents a landmark case in the history of cyber warfare, showcasing the use of a highly sophisticated and targeted cyber-weapon with specific objectives to physically damage industrial systems. The attack type associated with Stuxnet goes beyond traditional malware, emphasizing its unique nature as a cyber-physical weapon designed for strategic purposes.

4. Equifax Data Breach (2017):

The Equifax data breach in 2017 was a cyberattack that resulted in the unauthorized access and theft of sensitive personal information of approximately 147 million people. The attack was primarily characterized as a "data breach" and fell into the category of a large-scale, sophisticated cyber intrusion.

Here are key aspects and characteristics of the Equifax data breach:

Attack Type: Unauthorized Access and Data Breach

Description: Attackers exploited a vulnerability in the Apache Struts web application framework to gain unauthorized access to Equifax's systems. This breach exposed sensitive personal information of over 147 million individuals, including names, social security numbers, and credit card details. The incident highlighted the importance of patching known vulnerabilities promptly.

Unauthorized Access and Data Theft: The attackers gained unauthorized access to Equifax's systems, exploiting a vulnerability in Apache Struts, a popular open-source web application framework used by the company. Once inside, the attackers exfiltrated a vast amount of sensitive personal information, including names, Social Security numbers, birth dates, addresses, and, sometimes, driver's license numbers.

Exploitation of Software Vulnerability: The attackers exploited a known vulnerability in the Apache Struts software that Equifax was using. The vulnerability had a patch available, but Equifax failed to apply the patch promptly, leading to successful exploitation by the attackers.

The incident highlighted the importance of timely patching and vulnerability management in cybersecurity.

Prolonged Undetected Access: The attackers had unauthorized access to Equifax's systems for an extended period before the breach was discovered. The prolonged dwell time allowed the attackers to exfiltrate large amounts of sensitive data without detection. The delayed detection raised concerns about the effectiveness of Equifax's cybersecurity monitoring and incident response capabilities.

Scope and Scale: The Equifax data breach was one of the largest and most significant data breaches in history, affecting a massive number of individuals and exposing a wide range of sensitive personal information. The scale of the breach had significant implications for affected individuals, including the potential for identity theft and financial fraud.

Response and Public Disclosure: Equifax faced criticism for its handling of the breach, including delays in public disclosure and communication about the incident. The company provided credit monitoring services to affected individuals and took steps to enhance its cybersecurity measures following the breach.

Regulatory and Legal Consequences: The Equifax data breach resulted in regulatory scrutiny, investigations, and legal consequences for the company. Equifax faced legal action from individuals, regulators, and government entities, leading to settlements and fines related to the mishandling of the security incident.

Impact on Individuals and Credit Reporting: The exposure of sensitive personal information, including Social Security numbers and other identifying details, had a profound impact on the affected individuals. The breach raised concerns about the security of credit reporting agencies and the potential misuse of compromised information.

In summary, the Equifax data breach was a significant cybersecurity incident that exposed weaknesses in protecting sensitive personal information. It underscored the importance of timely patching, robust cybersecurity practices, and effective incident response to prevent and mitigate the impact of data breaches.

5. SolarWinds Supply Chain Attack (2020):

The SolarWinds supply chain attack, discovered in December 2020, was a highly sophisticated and widespread cyber espionage campaign. This attack is often characterized as a "supply chain compromise" or a "software supply chain attack." The attackers compromised the software supply chain by inserting a malicious backdoor into software updates provided by SolarWinds, a leading provider of IT management and monitoring software.

Here are key aspects and characteristics of the SolarWinds supply chain attack:

Attack Type: Software Supply Chain Compromise

Description: Malicious actors compromised the software build process of SolarWinds, a widely used IT management software provider. The attackers inserted a backdoor into the software updates, allowing them to conduct espionage activities across various government and private organizations. This incident emphasized the need to secure the software supply chain.

Compromise on Software Supply Chain: The attackers infiltrated the software build and distribution process of SolarWinds, a trusted software vendor. They introduced a backdoor into the Orion platform, a widely used IT infrastructure monitoring and management solution.

Distribution of Malicious Updates: The compromised software updates, containing the malicious backdoor, were signed with legitimate SolarWinds digital certificates. This allowed the malicious updates to appear authentic and trustworthy to users who received them.

Targeting High-Profile Organizations: The attackers targeted high-profile organizations, including government agencies, technology companies, and other critical infrastructure entities, by compromising the software used for monitoring and managing their IT environments.

SUNBURST (Solorigate) Malware: The backdoor introduced into the SolarWinds Orion platform was named "SUNBURST" or "Solorigate." This malware allowed the attackers to gain persistent access to the compromised networks and exfiltrate sensitive information.

Advanced Persistent Threat (APT) Attribution: The SolarWinds supply chain attack is attributed to an advanced, persistent threat group known as APT29 or Cozy Bear. APT29 is believed to be associated with Russian intelligence.

Silent and Covert Operation: The attack operated silently for an extended period, with the compromised updates being distributed to SolarWinds customers between March and June 2020. This prolonged dwelling time allowed the attackers to conduct reconnaissance, move laterally within networks, and handpick their targets.

Supply Chain Trust Exploitation: SolarWinds was a trusted supplier, and the attackers exploited this trust to distribute malicious updates. Organizations that regularly received and installed software updates from SolarWinds unknowingly introduced the backdoor into their environments.

Scope and Impact: The SolarWinds supply chain attack had a widespread impact, affecting thousands of SolarWinds customers globally. The compromised networks included government agencies, private companies, and organizations in various sectors, raising concerns about the potential theft of sensitive data and the compromise of national security.

Post-Compromise Activities: Following the initial compromise, the attackers engaged in post-compromise activities, including lateral movement, privilege escalation, and the exfiltration of sensitive information. The attackers showed a high level of sophistication and expertise in conducting covert and persistent cyber espionage.

Global Response and Mitigation: The discovery of the SolarWinds supply chain attack triggered a global response from cybersecurity experts, government agencies, and affected organizations. Mitigation efforts involved identifying and removing the compromised SolarWinds software, enhancing security measures, and conducting forensic investigations to understand the extent of the compromise.

In summary, the SolarWinds supply chain attack was a highly sophisticated and impactful cyber espionage campaign that exploited the trust associated with a trusted software vendor. The attack highlighted the vulnerability of software supply chains and the need for enhanced security measures to detect and prevent such threats.

6. Sony Pictures Hack (2014):

The Sony Pictures hack occurred in late 2014, and it was a cyberattack on Sony Pictures Entertainment, a division of Sony Corporation. The attackers, who identified themselves as the "Guardians of Peace," gained unauthorized access to Sony's computer systems, resulting in the theft of a large amount of sensitive and confidential data.

Here are key characteristics of the Sony Pictures Hack:

Attack Type: Data Breach and Destruction

Description: A group known as the Guardians of Peace (GOP) targeted Sony Pictures, leaking sensitive internal documents, unreleased films, and confidential emails. Attackers also deployed destructive malware that wiped data from Sony's network. The incident showcased the potential for cyberattacks to not only steal information but also to cause significant disruption and reputational damage. GOP claimed responsibility for the attack and demanded that Sony cancel the release of the film "The Interview," a satirical comedy about North Korea's leader, Kim Jong-un.

Motivation: The motivation behind the attack was initially unclear, but it was later believed to be in response to the upcoming release of "The Interview," which depicted a fictional assassination plot against the North Korea leader. The GOP expressed opposition to the film and threatened violence against theaters that screened it.

Consequences: The Sony Pictures hack had severe consequences for the company. It led to the leaking of sensitive information, damage to Sony's reputation, and financial losses. The incident highlighted the vulnerability of major corporations to cyber-attacks and raised concerns about cybersecurity in the entertainment industry.

Attribution: While the U.S. government attributed the attack on North Korea, there has been ongoing debate and skepticism about the true identity and motivations of the hackers. Some cybersecurity experts have questioned the official attribution.

In response to the incident, Sony Pictures took measures to enhance its cybersecurity infrastructure, and the broader industry became more vigilant regarding the potential for cyber threats.

7. Mirai Botnet (2016):

The Mirai botnet attack in 2016 was a large-scale and notable Distributed Denial of Service (DDoS) attack that exploited insecure Internet of Things (IoT) devices. The attack type associated with Mirai is specifically categorized as an "IoT botnet DDoS attack."

Here are key characteristics of the Mirai botnet attack:

Attack Type: Internet of Things (IoT) Exploitation

Description: The Mirai botnet targeted IoT devices, such as routers and cameras, by exploiting weak or default credentials. The compromised devices were then used to launch massive Distributed Denial of Service (DDoS) attacks. Mirai showed the vulnerabilities inherent in poorly secured IoT devices and the potential for creating large-scale botnets for cyberattacks.

IoT Device Exploitation: Mirai targeted a wide range of insecure IoT devices, including cameras, routers, and DVRs, which were commonly connected to the internet with default or weak credentials. The botnet recruited these compromised devices, turning them into remotely controlled bots.

Botnet Formation: Mirai malware scanned the internet for IoT devices with weak security, attempting to log in using a predefined list of common usernames and passwords. Once Mirai gained access to a device, it installed itself, creating a network of compromised devices that formed the Mirai botnet.

DDoS Attack Vector: The primary purpose of the Mirai botnet was to launch large-scale DDoS attacks. DDoS attacks overwhelm a target's online services by flooding them with a massive volume of traffic, making them unavailable to legitimate users. Mirai's DDoS attacks were powerful and had the potential to disrupt targeted websites, online services, and even entire networks.

High-Profile Targets: Mirai gained widespread attention because of its targeting of high-profile websites and services. Notable targets included the DNS service provider Dyn, leading to widespread internet outages and disruptions in October 2016. The attack showed the potential impact of exploiting insecure IoT devices on critical internet infrastructure.

Variants and Evolution: Mirai was just one of several IoT botnets, and its source code was eventually released online. This led to the creation of various Mirai variants and the emergence of new IoT botnets that used similar techniques. The proliferation of Mirai-inspired botnets highlighted the ongoing challenge of securing IoT devices and the potential for large-scale DDoS attacks.

Security Implications for IoT Devices: The Mirai attack underscored the security vulnerabilities associated with IoT devices, especially those that lacked proper security controls and were deployed with default credentials. The incident prompted increased awareness of the need for manufacturers and consumers to prioritize security in IoT devices.

Legislation and Industry Response: The Mirai botnet attack prompted legislative and industry responses aimed at improving the security of IoT devices. Efforts included the introduction of guidelines and standards for secure IoT device development and deployment. Security guidelines, such as changing default passwords and regularly updating device firmware, gained prominence in mitigating the risk of similar attacks.

In summary, the Mirai botnet attack of 2016 was a significant event in the cybersecurity landscape, highlighting the vulnerabilities associated with insecure IoT devices and their potential exploitation for large-scale DDoS attacks. The incident spurred efforts to improve IoT device security and mitigate the risks posed by botnets targeting connected devices.

8. Colonial Pipeline Ransomware Attack (2021):

The Colonial Pipeline ransomware attack in 2021 was a high-profile cyber incident characterized as a ransomware attack with potential implications for critical infrastructure.

Here are key aspects and characteristics of the Colonial Pipeline ransomware attack:

Attack Type: Ransomware

Description: The Colonial Pipeline, a critical infrastructure asset responsible for supplying fuel to the U.S. East Coast, become a victim to a ransomware attack. The attackers encrypted critical data, causing operational disruptions, and leading to the temporary shutdown of the pipeline. This incident highlighted the vulnerabilities of critical infrastructure to cyber threats.

Ransomware Attack: The attack involved the deployment of ransomware on Colonial Pipeline's computer systems. Ransomware is a type of malware that encrypts files or systems, rendering them inaccessible. The attackers then demand a ransom payment, typically in cryptocurrency, in exchange for providing the decryption key.

DarkSide Ransomware: The ransomware used in the Colonial Pipeline attack was identified as DarkSide, a type of ransomware known for targeting large organizations. DarkSide is often associated with ransomware-as-a-service (RaaS), where developers provide the ransomware to affiliates who carry out the attacks.

Critical Infrastructure Impact: Colonial Pipeline is a major energy infrastructure operator responsible for transporting a significant portion of the fuel supply along the East Coast of the United States. The attack had potential implications for critical infrastructure, as disruptions to fuel supply chains could affect the economy and public services.

Impact on Operations: The attack forced the Colonial Pipeline to shut down its operations temporarily to prevent the spread of the ransomware and assess the extent of the compromise. The shutdown of the pipeline led to concerns about fuel shortages, and it highlighted the vulnerabilities of critical infrastructure to cyber threats.

Ransom Payment Controversy: Colonial Pipeline faced a tough decision regarding whether to pay the ransom to expedite the recovery of its systems and resume operations. Ultimately, the company confirmed making a ransom payment of approximately 75 Bitcoin (equivalent to millions of dollars) to the attackers.

Federal Response and Investigation: The attack prompted a response from various federal agencies, including the Federal Bureau of Investigation (FBI) and the Department of Homeland Security (DHS). The incident raised concerns about the potential national security implications of cyberattacks on critical infrastructure.

Supply Chain Security Concerns: The Colonial Pipeline attack raised awareness about the broader issue of supply chain security, as attackers exploited vulnerabilities in the pipeline operator's IT systems to affect the physical delivery of fuel. It emphasized the need for enhanced cybersecurity measures throughout the supply chain, especially in critical infrastructure sectors.

Increased Cybersecurity Awareness: The incident increased awareness about the importance of robust cybersecurity practices in critical infrastructure and the potential cascading effects of cyber disruptions on various sectors of the economy.

The Colonial Pipeline ransomware attack highlighted the significant impact that cyber threats can have on critical infrastructure, leading to increased attention on securing essential services and supply chains against cyber threats. It also sparked discussions about the role of cybersecurity regulations, incident response, and information sharing in safeguarding critical infrastructure from growing cyber risk.

XI. CYBER HYGIENE MATTERS

As we navigate the complex landscape of active cyberattacks, several important points emerge: "Cyber hygiene" refers to the set of practices and measures that individuals and organizations adopt to maintain good cybersecurity health. It involves taking active steps to protect digital systems, networks, and data from cyber threats.

Just as personal hygiene helps prevent illness and maintain well-being, cyber hygiene is essential for safeguarding against cyberattacks and maintaining the overall health of information systems. Regular software updates, strong password policies, and secure configurations form the foundation of effective cyber hygiene. Neglecting these basics can create vulnerabilities that adversaries are quick to exploit.

Here are key aspects and details about why cyber hygiene matters:

1. Preventing Common Cyber Threats:

1.1. Malware and Ransomware: Regularly updating software, using reputable antivirus programs, and being cautious about email attachments can help prevent malware infections and ransomware attacks.

1.2. Phishing Attacks: Recognizing phishing emails, avoiding clicking on suspicious links, and verifying the legitimacy of communications can prevent falling victim to phishing attacks.

2. Protecting Personal and Sensitive Information:

2.1. Strong Passwords: Creating and regularly updating strong, unique passwords for different accounts helps protect personal and sensitive information from unauthorized access.

2.2. Two-Factor Authentication (2FA): Enabling 2FA adds an extra layer of security by requiring a second form of verification beyond just a password.

3. Securing Devices and Networks:

3.1. Software Updates: Keeping operating systems, software, and applications up to date with the latest security patches is crucial for closing vulnerabilities and reducing the risk of exploitation.

3.2. Firewalls and Antivirus Software: Using firewalls and reliable antivirus software helps protect devices from unauthorized access and malicious software.

4. Data Backups and Recovery:

4.1. Regular Backups: Creating regular backups of important data ensures that, in the event of a cyber incident or data loss, information can be recovered without paying a ransom or facing significant disruptions.

4.2. Testing Backup Restoration: Periodically testing the restoration process of backups ensures their integrity and usability when needed.

5. Employee Training and Awareness:

5.1. Cybersecurity Training: Providing employees with cybersecurity training helps them recognize and respond to potential threats, reducing the likelihood of falling victim to social engineering attacks.

5.2. Security Awareness Programs: Regularly updating employees on the latest cyber threats and promoting a security-conscious culture can enhance overall cybersecurity awareness.

6. Mobile Device Security:

6.1. Device Locks and Encryption: Implementing locks on mobile devices and enabling encryption adds an extra layer of protection to prevent unauthorized access to sensitive information.

6.2. App Permissions: Reviewing and limiting app permissions on mobile devices helps control the access apps have to personal data.

7. Incident Response Planning:

7.1. Developing a Response Plan: Having a well-defined incident response plan in place helps organizations respond effectively to cyber incidents, minimizing damage and downtime.

7.2. Regular Drills and Testing: Conducting regular drills and testing the incident response plan ensures that the organization is prepared to handle different cyber threat types.

8. Compliance with Regulations:

8.1. Data Protection Laws: Adhering to data protection regulations and industry-specific compliance requirements is essential for avoiding legal consequences and protecting sensitive information.

8.2. Privacy and Consent: Respecting user privacy, getting consent for data collection, and being transparent about how data is used contribute to ethical cybersecurity practices.

9. Continuous Monitoring and Assessment:

9.1. Security Audits and Assessments: Regularly conducting security audits and assessments helps identify vulnerabilities, assess risks, and implement necessary security improvements.

9.2. Monitoring Network Traffic: Continuous monitoring of network traffic enables the detection of suspicious activities and potential security incidents in real-time.

10. Collaboration and Information Sharing:

10.1. Threat Intelligence Sharing: taking part in threat intelligence sharing communities allows organizations to stay informed about emerging cyber threats and adopt an active measure.

10.2. Collaboration with Peers: Sharing insights and guidelines with industry peers contributes to collective efforts in enhancing cybersecurity resilience.

In summary, cyber hygiene is foundational to effective cybersecurity. By adopting and consistently practicing good cyber hygiene habits, individuals and organizations can reduce the risk of falling victim to cyber threats, protect sensitive information, and contribute to a more secure digital environment. Regular software updates, awareness, and an active approach to cybersecurity are critical components of maintaining strong cyber hygiene.

XII. HUMAN ELEMENT CANNOT BE IGNORED

Education and awareness are critical components of cyber defense. The examples of phishing and social engineering highlight the need for ongoing training to empower individuals to recognize and resist manipulation.

The human element is a critical and often underestimated factor within the realm of cybersecurity. While technological solutions, policies, and procedures are essential, the actions and behaviors of individuals, both malicious actors and well-intentioned users, play a significant role in the success or failure of cybersecurity measures.

Here, in emphasizing why the human element cannot be ignored in cyberattacks:

1. Social Engineering Attacks:

1.1. Phishing: Social engineering attacks, such as phishing, rely on manipulating individuals to divulge sensitive information or perform actions that compromise security. Phishing emails often impersonate trusted entities, exploiting human trust and curiosity.

1.2. Pretexting: Attackers may create false scenarios (pretexts) to trick individuals into providing information or performing actions they wouldn't normally do.

2. Insider Threats:

2.1. Malicious Insiders: Employees or individuals with insider access can intentionally or unintentionally compromise security. Malicious insiders may exploit their access for personal gain or act as unwitting accomplices to external threats.

2.2. Unintentional Mistakes: Well-intentioned employees may inadvertently introduce security risks through actions like misconfigurations, accidental data exposure, or falling victim to social engineering.

3. Security Awareness and Training:

3.1. Human Error Mitigation: Investing in cybersecurity awareness programs and training helps educate individuals about the latest threats, guidelines, and how to recognize and respond to potential risks.

3.2. Phishing Simulations: Regularly conducting phishing simulations allows organizations to assess the susceptibility of employees to phishing attacks and tailor training accordingly.

4. Authentication and Access Control:

4.1. Password Management: Weak passwords and poor password management practices can be exploited. Encouraging strong, unique passwords and implementing multi-factor authentication (MFA) enhances access control.

4.2. Role-Based Access Control (RBAC): Limiting access privileges based on job roles helps minimize the risk associated with insider threats.

5. Cultural and Organizational Factors:

5.1. Security Culture: Establishing a strong security culture within an organization fosters a collective understanding and commitment to cybersecurity. This includes promoting a sense of responsibility for security among all employees.

5.2. Leadership Commitment: Leadership plays a crucial role in setting the tone for cybersecurity. When leaders prioritize and champion security initiatives, it encourages a more security-conscious culture.

6. Remote Work Challenges:

6.1. Remote Access Security: The rise of remote work introduces new challenges, with employees accessing corporate networks from various locations and devices. Ensuring secure remote access requires addressing human behaviors, such as connecting to unsecured networks.

6.2. Phishing Targeting Remote Workers: Cybercriminals have exploited the shift to remote work by launching targeted phishing attacks that leverage the unique circumstances and concerns of remote workers.

7. User-Centric Design:

7.1. Usability and Security Balance: Security measures must be designed with user experience in mind. Overly complex or restrictive security measures may lead to circumvention by users, emphasizing the need for a balance between usability and security.

7.2. User-Friendly Security Tools: Intuitive and user-friendly security tools are more likely to be embraced and used effectively by individuals, reducing the likelihood of security gaps.

8. Incident Response and Reporting:

8.1. Reporting Culture: Establishing a culture where individuals feel comfortable reporting potential security incidents or concerns is crucial for early detection and response.

8.2. Incident Response Training: Regular training on incident response procedures ensures employees know how to report incidents promptly, facilitating a swift and effective response.

9. Human-Centric Threat Detection:

9.1. Behavioral Analytics: Human-centric threat detection involves analyzing user behavior for anomalies that may show malicious activity. Behavioral analytics can help identify deviations from normal patterns, signaling potential security incidents.

9.2. User Behavior Monitoring: Continuous monitoring of user behavior can aid in the early detection of insider threats or compromised accounts.

10. Privacy and Ethical Considerations:

10.1. Balancing Security and Privacy: Organizations need to consider both security and privacy concerns. Implementing security measures must be done in a way that respects individual privacy rights and ethical considerations.

10.2. Ethical Hacking and Red Teaming: Ethical hacking and red teaming exercises involve simulating cyberattacks to identify vulnerabilities and weaknesses. These exercises often incorporate the human element to test both technical and human defenses.

In conclusion, the human element is an integral part of the cybersecurity landscape. Effective cybersecurity strategies recognize the importance of human behaviors, both as potential vulnerabilities and as crucial components of a resilient defense. Combining technological solutions with ongoing education, awareness, and a user-centric approach enhances an organization's ability to protect against growing cyber threats. Ignoring the human element can leave significant gaps in cybersecurity defenses and undermine overall resilience.

XIII. COLLABORATION IS KEY

Cyber threats transcend borders, making international collaboration essential. Sharing threat intelligence, guidelines, and collectively addressing vulnerabilities contribute to a more secure digital ecosystem. Collaboration is a key principle in cybersecurity, emphasizing the importance of collective efforts among individuals, organizations, and communities to enhance overall cyber resilience.

Cyber threats are dynamic, growing, and often transcend organizational boundaries. Effective collaboration fosters information sharing, joint defense efforts, and a united front against cyber adversaries.

These detailed aspects underscore the significance of collaboration in cybersecurity.

1. Threat Intelligence Sharing:

1.1. Real-Time Threat Awareness: Collaborative sharing of threat intelligence allows organizations to stay informed about the latest cyber threats, attack techniques, and indicators of compromise (IOCs) in real-time.

1.2. Active Defense: Armed with timely threat intelligence, organizations can proactively adjust their cybersecurity measures to counter emerging threats before they become widespread.

2. Industry Information Sharing:

2.1. Cross-Sector Collaboration: Collaboration across different industries facilitates the sharing of sector-specific threat insights and guidelines. What affects one sector may have implications for others, and cross-industry collaboration strengthens collective defenses.

2.2. Joint Response to Common Threats: Industry-specific Information Sharing and Analysis Centers (ISACs) or Information Sharing and Analysis Organizations (ISAOs) enable organizations within a sector to collaborate on cybersecurity issues.

3. Public-Private Partnerships:

3.1. Government and Private Sector Collaboration: Collaborative efforts between government agencies and private sector organizations enhance the overall cybersecurity posture. Government agencies can provide threat intelligence, regulatory guidance, and support, while private sector entities contribute expertise and insights.

3.2. Critical Infrastructure Protection: Public-private partnerships are crucial for protecting critical infrastructure, ensuring coordinated responses to cyber threats that could affect national security and public safety.

4. International Cooperation:

4.1. Global Threat Landscape: Cyber threats often have international dimensions. Collaborating on a global scale allows for a more comprehensive understanding of the threat landscape and facilitates joint responses to transnational cybercrime.

4.2. Information Exchange: International collaboration involves sharing information and guidelines across borders, promoting a united effort against cyber adversaries.

5. Incident Response Coordination:

5.1. Coordination Among Stakeholders: In the event of a cyber incident, effective collaboration is critical for coordinated incident response efforts. This involves collaboration between internal teams, external partners, law enforcement, and relevant regulatory bodies.

5.2. Information Sharing During Incidents: Timely and accurate sharing of information about ongoing incidents enables a more effective response, containment, and recovery.

6. Vendor and Supplier Collaboration:

6.1. Supply Chain Security: Collaborating with vendors and suppliers is essential for ensuring the security of the supply chain. This involves establishing security standards, conducting assessments, and promoting secure development practices.

6.2. Vendor Risk Management: Organizations need to work collaboratively with their vendors to assess and manage cybersecurity risks, ensuring that the entire supply chain is resilient to cyber threats.

7. Community Engagement:

7.1. Educational Initiatives: Collaborative efforts in cybersecurity education and awareness help empower individuals and organizations with the knowledge to defend against cyber threats.

7.2. Community-Based Defense: Local communities and organizations can collaborate on cybersecurity initiatives, sharing resources and expertise to create a more secure environment for everyone.

8. Sharing Guidelines:

8.1. Knowledge Exchange: Collaboration facilitates the exchange of guidelines and lessons learned. Organizations can learn from each other's experiences, successes, and challenges, leading to continuous improvement in cybersecurity strategies.

8.2. Industry Standard Development: Collaborative efforts contribute to the development of industry standards and frameworks that enhance the consistency and effectiveness of cybersecurity practices.

9. Crisis Communication:

9.1. Communication Channels: Establishing effective communication channels is crucial for sharing information during a cybersecurity crisis. Collaborative efforts ensure relevant stakeholders are kept informed in a timely and transparent manner.

9.2. Joint Messaging: Consistent and coordinated messaging across organizations and sectors helps prevent misinformation and confusion during a cyber incident.

10. Multi-Stakeholder Engagement:

10.1. Inclusive Collaboration: Engaging a diverse range of stakeholders, including government, industry, academia, and civil society, promotes inclusive collaboration. Different perspectives contribute to a more comprehensive and resilient cybersecurity ecosystem.

10.2. Shared Responsibility: Recognizing that cybersecurity is a shared responsibility encourages active participation and commitment from all stakeholders, fostering a culture of collective defense.

In summary, collaboration is a linchpin in building effective cybersecurity defenses. The interconnected and growing nature of cyber threats causes a collaborative approach that leverages collective intelligence, resources, and expertise. By working together, stakeholders can create a more robust and adaptive cybersecurity environment, better equipped to address the challenges posed by a dynamic and rapidly changing threat landscape.

XIV. SUPPLY CHAIN SECURITY IS PARAMOUNT

The SolarWinds incident showed the cascading impact of a supply chain compromise. Organizations must scrutinize and fortify their software supply chains to prevent malicious actors from exploiting trusted channels. Supply chain security is paramount in cybersecurity because of the interconnected and interdependent nature of modern supply chains.

Organizations rely on a complex network of suppliers, vendors, manufacturers, and service providers to deliver goods and services. However, this interconnectedness introduces cybersecurity risks, as vulnerabilities in one part of the supply chain might affect the entire ecosystem.

These detailed aspects underline the importance of supply chain security in cybersecurity.

1. Attack Surface Expansion:

1.1. Extended Attack Surface: A supply chain involves multiple entities, each representing a potential entry point for cyber attackers. A compromise in any part of the supply chain can lead to broader security implications for downstream organizations.

1.2. Third-Party Risk: Organizations often share sensitive information with suppliers and service providers. If these third parties are not adequately secured, they become potential targets, exposing the organization to additional risks.

2. Dependency on Third-Party Software and Components:

2.1. Software and Hardware Supply Chain: Organizations often rely on third-party software, hardware, and components. Malicious actors can target the supply chain to inject vulnerabilities or backdoors into products, which may go undetected until later stages.

2.2. Open-Source Software Risks: The use of open-source software introduces additional challenges, as organizations may inherit vulnerabilities from third-party code that is integrated into their products or systems.

3. Counterfeit and Tampering Risks:

3.1. Counterfeit Products: Insecure supply chains can expose organizations to counterfeit hardware or software, which may have compromised functionality or hidden malicious components.

3.2. Tampering with Products: The physical supply chain is susceptible to tampering, where malicious actors may compromise products during transportation or storage, leading to potential security breaches.

4. Regulatory Compliance and Legal Consequences:

4.1. Data Protection and Privacy Laws: Regulatory frameworks often hold organizations responsible for protecting customer data. A security breach originating from the supply chain may cause legal consequences and regulatory fines.

4.2. Contractual Obligations: Organizations may have contractual obligations to safeguard the data and assets of their customers. Supply chain compromises can lead to breaches of these contractual agreements.

5. Business Continuity and Resilience:

5.1. Disruption Potential: A security incident in the supply chain, such as a ransomware attack on a key supplier, can disrupt operations and affect the availability of goods and services.

5.2. Resilience Planning: Supply chain security is integral to business continuity and resilience planning. Organizations must assess and mitigate risks to ensure uninterrupted operations even in the face of supply chain disruptions.

6. Intellectual Property Protection:

6.1. Trade Secrets and Innovation: Organizations invest heavily in research and development. Insecure supply chains may expose proprietary information and trade secrets, compromising an organization's point of difference and innovation.

6.2. Protecting Intellectual Property: Ensuring the security of the supply chain is essential for protecting intellectual property and maintaining a competitive edge in the market.

7. Supplier and Vendor Risk Management:

7.1. Assessing Supplier Security Practices: Organizations need to assess the cybersecurity practices of their suppliers and vendors. This includes evaluating their security policies, incident response capabilities, and overall cybersecurity posture.

7.2. Supplier Security Audits: Conducting regular security audits of suppliers and vendors helps verify their adherence to security standards and compliance requirements.

8. Cybersecurity Due Diligence:

8.1. Due Diligence in Mergers and Acquisitions: During mergers and acquisitions, organizations need to conduct thorough cybersecurity due diligence on the target company's supply chain to identify potential risks and liabilities.

8.2. Ongoing Monitoring: Cybersecurity due diligence should be an ongoing process, especially as the supply chain grows and unknown risks emerge.

9. Collaboration and Information Sharing:

9.1. Industry Collaboration: Collaborative efforts within industries can enhance supply chain security. Sharing threat intelligence, guidelines, and lessons learned helps strengthen the collective defense against common threats.

9.2. Information Sharing Platforms: Establishing platforms for sharing information about supply chain threats and vulnerabilities allows organizations to stay informed and respond more effectively to emerging risks.

10. Continuous Monitoring and Incident Response:

10.1. Real-Time Monitoring: Continuous monitoring of the supply chain enables organizations to detect anomalies, suspicious activities, and potential security incidents in real time.

10.2. Rapid Incident Response: Having effective incident response mechanisms in place ensures swift action to contain and mitigate the impact of security incidents on the supply chain.

11. Cybersecurity Standards and Frameworks:

11.1. Adherence to Standards: Following established cybersecurity standards and frameworks, such as ISO 27001, the NIST Cybersecurity Framework, or others, provides a structured approach to securing the supply chain.

11.2. Certifications and Compliance: Ensuring that suppliers and vendors adhere to recognized cybersecurity standards through certifications and compliance measures helps raise the overall security posture of the supply chain.

12. Employee Training and Awareness:

12.1. Supply Chain Security Education: Training employees on supply chain security risks and guidelines ensures they are aware of their role in maintaining a secure supply chain.

12.2. Security Awareness Programs: Ongoing security awareness programs help employees recognize and report potential threats and vulnerabilities within the supply chain.

In conclusion, supply chain security is a critical component of a comprehensive cybersecurity strategy. Organizations must recognize the importance of securing their supply chains to protect against a wide range of cyber threats and to maintain the trust of customers, partners, and stakeholders. By implementing robust supply chain security measures, organizations can build resilience, reduce vulnerabilities, and strengthen their overall cybersecurity posture.

XV. RESILIENCE AND INCIDENT RESPONSE ARE ESSENTIAL

No defense is foolproof. A robust incident response plan, including regular drills, ensures a swift and effective response when an active cyberattack occurs. The ability to recover quickly is as crucial as preventing the attack itself. Resilience and incident response are essential components of an effective cybersecurity strategy. These elements focus on an organization's ability to withstand and recover from cybersecurity incidents, ensuring continuity of operations, and minimizing the impact of potential threats.

These detailed aspects emphasize the importance of resilience and incident response in cybersecurity.

1. Active Cybersecurity Resilience:

1.1. Risk Assessment and Management: Proactively identifying and assessing cybersecurity risks allows organizations to implement measures to enhance resilience against potential threats.

1.2. Resilience Planning: Developing a cybersecurity resilience plan involves preparing for potential incidents, defining roles and responsibilities, and establishing communication channels to ensure a coordinated response.

2. Continuous Monitoring and Threat Detection:

2.1. Real-Time Monitoring: Continuous monitoring of networks, systems, and applications enables the early detection of suspicious activities, potential vulnerabilities, or signs of cyber intrusion.

2.2. Threat Intelligence Integration: Incorporating threat intelligence into monitoring efforts enhances the ability to identify emerging threats and understand the tactics, techniques, and procedures (TTPs) employed by cyber adversaries.

3. Incident Response Readiness:

3.1. Incident Response Plan: Having a well-defined incident response plan is essential. This plan outlines the steps to be taken when a cybersecurity incident occurs, including communication protocols, roles, and procedures for investigation and recovery.

3.2. Tabletop Exercises: Conducting tabletop exercises simulates real-world cyber incidents and allow organizations to test their incident response capabilities, identify weaknesses, and refine their response procedures.

4. Communication and Coordination:

4.1. Communication Protocols: Establishing clear communication protocols ensures that all relevant stakeholders are informed promptly in the event of a cybersecurity incident.

4.2. Coordination Among Teams: Effective incident response requires coordination among various teams, including IT, security, legal, public relations, and executive leadership.

5. Forensic Analysis and Investigation:

5.1. Forensic Capabilities: Building forensic capabilities enables organizations to conduct thorough investigations into cybersecurity incidents, understand the root causes, and gather evidence for legal or regulatory purposes.

5.2. Preserving Digital Evidence: Properly preserving digital evidence is crucial for identifying the extent of a security incident and supporting any subsequent legal or law enforcement actions.

6. Containment and Mitigation:

6.1. Rapid Response: A well-prepared incident response plan allows organizations to respond rapidly to contain and mitigate the impact of a cybersecurity incident.

6.2. Isolation and Quarantine: Implementing measures to isolate affected systems or networks helps prevent the spread of malware or unauthorized access during an incident.

7. Business Continuity and Recovery:

7.1. Resilient Infrastructure: Building resilient IT infrastructure, including redundant systems and data backups, ensures that critical operations can continue even in the face of disruptions.

7.2. Backup and Recovery Procedures: Regularly testing backup and recovery procedures ensures organizations can restore operations quickly following a cybersecurity incident.

8. Post-Incident Analysis and Improvement:

8.1. After-Action Reviews: Conducting after-action reviews allows organizations to analyze their response to a cybersecurity incident, identify areas for improvement, and update incident response plans accordingly.

8.2. Continuous Improvement: The lessons learned from incidents should inform ongoing cybersecurity efforts, including updates on policies, procedures, and security controls.

9. Regulatory Compliance and Reporting:

9.1. Regulatory Obligations: Many industries have regulatory requirements for incident reporting and response. Compliance with these regulations is essential to avoid legal consequences and financial penalties.

9.2. Timely Reporting: Promptly reporting incidents to regulatory authorities, customers, and affected parties is critical for transparency and compliance with data protection laws.

10. User Training and Awareness:

10.1. Security Education: Training employees on cybersecurity guidelines and incident response procedures helps create a security-conscious culture.

10.2. Incident Reporting: Encouraging a culture of reporting potential incidents ensures employees are actively involved in early detection and response efforts.

11. Redundancy and Failover Systems:

11.1. Redundant Systems: Implementing redundant systems and failover mechanisms enhances resilience by ensuring that critical functions can continue even if primary systems are compromised.

11.2. Cloud-Based Services: Leveraging cloud-based services for redundancy and data storage can contribute to a more resilient infrastructure.

12. Legal and Public Relations Preparedness:

12.1. Legal Counsel Involvement: Involving legal counsel in incident response planning ensures that organizations are prepared for potential legal ramifications and can navigate legal considerations during and after an incident.

12.2. Public Relations Strategy: Having a public relations strategy in place helps manage the organization's public image and communication during and after a cybersecurity incident, reducing reputational damage.

In conclusion, cybersecurity resilience and incident response are essential elements of a comprehensive cybersecurity strategy. By building resilience, organizations can better withstand and recover from cyber threats, and by implementing effective incident response measures, they can minimize the impact of incidents when they occur. Continuous improvement, collaboration, and an active approach to cybersecurity are key to successfully navigating the growing threat landscape.

The battle against active cyberattacks is ongoing, dynamic, and requires a multi-faceted approach. By embracing a culture of cybersecurity, investing in advanced technologies, and fostering collaboration, we can collectively strive to outsmart and outpace the unseen adversaries that lurk in the digital shadows.

The growing nature of cyber threats causes constant adaptation, a commitment to innovation, education, and collaboration that will fortify our defenses and enable us to face the challenges of the digital age with resilience and determination.

XVI. ESSENTIAL CYBERSECURITY PRACTICES

Essential cybersecurity practices refer to a set of fundamental and active measures that organizations and individuals should implement to protect their digital assets, data, and systems from cyber threats. These practices are designed to establish a strong security foundation, reduce vulnerabilities, and mitigate the risk of cyberattacks. Essential cybersecurity practices encompass a range of activities, including prevention, detection, response, and recovery.

Here's an expanded definition of essential cybersecurity practices:

1. Risk Assessment:

1.1. Comprehensive Analysis: Conduct a comprehensive analysis of potential cybersecurity risks, considering factors such as the organization's assets, vulnerabilities, threats, and the potential impact of security incidents.

1.2. Regular Updates: Keep the risk assessment process updated regularly to adapt to changes in the organization's technology landscape and growing cyber threats.

2. Security Policies and Governance:

2.1. Policy Development: Develop clear and concise security policies covering areas such as data protection, acceptable use, password management, and incident response.

2.2. Governance Framework: Establish a governance framework that outlines how security policies will be enforced, monitored, and updated to align with organizational goals and compliance requirements.

3. User Training and Awareness:

3.1. Regular Training Sessions: Conduct regular training sessions to educate users about the latest cybersecurity threats, social engineering tactics, and guidelines for maintaining security.

3.2. Simulated Phishing Exercises: Implement simulated phishing exercises to assess and improve users' ability to recognize and respond to phishing attempts.

4. Access Control:

4.1. Principle of Least Privilege: Adhere to the principle of least privilege, granting users the minimum level of access necessary to perform their roles.

4.2. Regular Access Reviews: Conduct regular access reviews to ensure that user permissions align with their current responsibilities and revoke unnecessary privileges.

5. Regular Software Updates and Patch Management:

5.1. Automated Patching: Implement automated patch management tools to ensure timely installation of security patches across all systems.

5.2. Vulnerability Scanning: Regularly conduct vulnerability scanning to identify systems that require patching and prioritize remediation based on the severity of vulnerabilities.

6. Endpoint Protection:

6.1. Antivirus and Anti-Malware Solutions: Deploy and regularly update antivirus and anti-malware solutions on endpoints to detect and prevent malicious software.

6.2. Behavioral Analysis: Use advanced endpoint protection solutions that employ behavioral analysis to identify and stop malicious activities.

7. Firewalls and Network Security:

7.1. Intrusion Detection and Prevention Systems (IDPS): Implement IDPS to detect and respond to potential intrusions by analyzing network traffic patterns.

7.2. Regular Firewall Rule Reviews: Conduct regular reviews of firewall rules to ensure they align with security policies and only permit necessary traffic.

8. Encryption:

8.1. Data-in-Transit Encryption: Use secure protocols (e.g., TLS) to encrypt data transmitted over networks to protect against eavesdropping.

8.2. Data-at-Rest Encryption: Implement encryption for data stored on servers, databases, and other storage devices to prevent unauthorized access in case of physical or digital breaches.

9. Incident Response Plan:

9.1. Incident Categorization: Categorize and prioritize incidents based on severity, impact, and the level of risk to the organization.

9.2. Communication Protocols: Establish clear communication protocols, including designated channels for reporting incidents, both internally and externally.

10. Backup and Recovery:

10.1. Regular Backup Schedule: Establish a regular schedule for data backups, considering the criticality of data and the frequency of changes.

10.2. Testing Restoration: Periodically test the restoration process to ensure the integrity and availability of backups.

11. Multi-Factor Authentication (MFA):

11.1. Authentication Factors: Implement MFA using multiple factors, such as passwords, biometrics, or onetime codes, to enhance access security.

11.2. MFA for Critical Systems: Prioritize the use of MFA for access to critical systems, sensitive data, and privileged accounts.

12. Security Audits and Monitoring:

12.1. Real-Time Monitoring: Implement real-time monitoring of network traffic, system logs, and security alerts to detect and respond promptly to anomalies.

12.2. Security Information and Event Management (SIEM): Use SIEM solutions to aggregate and analyze security data for active threat detection.

13. Vulnerability Management:

13.1. Regular Vulnerability Scans: Conduct regular vulnerability scans to identify weaknesses in systems and applications.
13.2. Patch or Mitigate: Prioritize and apply patches or mitigations based on the severity of vulnerabilities to reduce the risk of exploitation.

14. Secure Configuration Practices:

14.1. Baseline Configurations: Establish secure baseline configurations for operating systems, applications, and network devices.

14.2. Regular Configuration Audits: Conduct regular audits to ensure that systems adhere to secure configuration practices.

15. Security Awareness for Development Teams:

15.1. Secure Coding Training: Provide ongoing training for software development teams on secure coding practices and common vulnerabilities.

15.2. Code Reviews: Incorporate security code reviews into the development process to identify and remediate security issues early.

16. Third-Party Security Assessments:

16.1. Vendor Risk Assessments: Regularly assess the security posture of third-party vendors, suppliers, and partners.

16.2. Contractual Security Requirements: Include security requirements in contracts with third parties to ensure they meet the organization's cybersecurity standards.

17. Cloud Security Best Practices:

17.1 Identity and Access Management (IAM): Implement strong IAM practices in cloud environments to control access to resources.

17.2. Encryption and Key Management: Use encryption and key management.

Essential cybersecurity practices form the foundation of a robust cybersecurity framework, providing organizations with the tools and strategies to navigate the complex and dynamic landscape of cyber threats. Implementing these practices helps build resilience, protect critical assets, and contributes to a more secure digital environment.

XVII. CONCLUSION

The battle against active cyberattacks is an ever-growing challenge that demands a strategic and multifaceted approach. In the dynamic landscape of cybersecurity, the adversary is unseen, agile, and constantly seeking new avenues of exploitation. To effectively counteract these threats, it is imperative to adopt a holistic mindset that encompasses a culture of cybersecurity, investment in advanced technologies, and collaborative efforts across the digital ecosystem.

Foremost, fostering a culture of cybersecurity within an organization is the bedrock of an effective defense strategy. This involves instilling a shared responsibility for security among all employees, from the boardroom to the front lines. Employees must be educated on the latest cyber threats, social engineering tactics, and guidelines for maintaining a secure digital environment. A security-conscious culture creates a human firewall, where individuals become active participants in the defense against cyber adversaries, recognizing the pivotal role each member plays in safeguarding the organization's assets.

In tandem with cultural awareness, investment in advanced cybersecurity technologies is paramount. The adversaries operate on the forefront of technology, and defenders must harness innovative tools to stay ahead. Deploying robust endpoint protection, intrusion detection systems, and advanced threat intelligence solutions enhances the organization's ability to detect, respond to, and mitigate cyber threats.

Machine learning and artificial intelligence play pivotal roles in augmenting human capabilities, providing real-time analysis of vast datasets and identifying patterns indicative of malicious activities. As the digital landscape grows, so must our technological defenses, ensuring they remain resilient against sophisticated cyber threats.

Collaboration emerges as a force multiplier in the battle against cyber adversaries. No organization is an island, and the sharing of threat intelligence, guidelines, and insights is crucial. Collaboration extends beyond organizational boundaries, involving public-private partnerships, industry alliances, and information-sharing platforms. By sharing knowledge about emerging threats and attack methodologies, the cybersecurity community can collectively bolster its defenses. This collaborative approach also extends to incident response, where organizations coordinate efforts to contain and neutralize threats swiftly, minimizing the impact of cyber incidents.

In conclusion, the battle against active cyberattacks causes a comprehensive and collaborative strategy. Fostering a culture of cybersecurity instills a sense of shared responsibility among individuals, creating a formidable human firewall. Concurrently, investing in advanced technologies empowers defenders with the tools needed to detect and respond to growing threats.

Finally, collaboration amplifies the collective strength of the cybersecurity community, enabling organizations to outsmart and outpace unseen adversaries in the ever-shifting digital landscape.

This multi-faceted approach is not merely a response; it is an active stance that ensures organizations are resilient, adaptive, and ready to face the challenges of the digital era.

XVII. FURTHER LEARNING RESOURCES

1. General Cybersecurity Learning Platforms:

- Cybrary
- Coursera - Cybersecurity Specializations
- edX - Cybersecurity Courses
- Udemy - Cybersecurity Courses
- SANS Institute
- Pluralsight - Cybersecurity Paths

2. Threat Intelligence and Analysis:

- MITRE ATT&CK Framework
- Cyber Threat Intelligence (CTI) League
- Open-Source Intelligence (OSINT) Framework

3. Penetration Testing and Ethical Hacking:

- Offensive Security - Certified Ethical Hacker (CEH)
- Hack The Box
- Metasploit Unleashed

4. Digital Forensics and Incident Response:

- Digital Forensics and Incident Response (DFIR) Resources
- SANS Digital Forensics and Incident Response

5. Cryptography:

- Khan Academy–Cryptography

6. Web Application Security:

- OWASP - Open Web Application Security Project
- PortSwigger Web Security Academy

7. Cloud Security:

- AWS Training and Certification
- Google Cloud Training
- Microsoft Learn - Azure Security

8. Mobile Security:

- Android Developers – Security
- iOS Security Guide

9. Networking and Infrastructure Security:

- Cisco Networking Academy
- CompTIA Network+ Training

10. Blogs and News:

- Krebs on Security
- The Hacker News
- Schneier on Security

11. Capture The Flag (CTF) Platforms:

- Hack The Box
- TryHackMe
- OverTheWire

12. YouTube Channels:

- https://www.youtube.com/@kgvconsulting-cybersecurity
- Hak5
- Cyber Mentor
- LiveOverflow

13. Podcasts:

- Darknet Diaries
- Security Now

14. Online Communities:

- Reddit - r/netsec
- Stack Exchange - Information Security

15. Certification Bodies:

- CompTIA
- ISC² - Certified Information Systems Security Professional (CISSP)
- EC-Council - Certified Ethical Hacker (CEH)

16. Open-Source Tools and Frameworks:

- OWASP GitHub Repository
- Snort - Open-Source IDS/IPS

17. Virtual Labs and Environments:

- Virtual Hacking Labs
- Pentester Academy

18. Books (Selected Titles):

- "The Web Application Hacker's Handbook" by Dafydd Stuttard and Marcus Pinto
- "Hacking: The Art of Exploitation" by Jon Erickson
- "Metasploit: The Penetration Tester's Guide" by David Kennedy, Jim O'Gorman, Devon Kearns, and Mati Aharoni
- "Practical Malware Analysis" by Michael Sikorski and Andrew Honig

19. Online Courses (Selected):

- Stanford University - Computer and Network Security

- MIT OpenCourseWare - Introduction to Computer Science and Programming in Python

Remember to choose resources based on your current skill level and areas of interest. Continuous learning and hands-on practice are key in the ever-growing field of cybersecurity.

ABOUT THE AUTHOR

With over 35 years in the field, I've immersed myself in Entrepreneurship, Cyber Security, and Software Development. As an entrepreneur, I've founded successful ventures, blending vision with strategic decisions. In Cyber Security, I've safeguarded digital landscapes with proactive measures. In Software Development, my expertise lies in crafting scalable and innovative solutions. I'm passionate about mentoring, sharing knowledge, and fostering growth. My journey reflects a commitment to continuous learning and making a positive impact in dynamic professional arenas.

www.ingramcontent.com/pod-product-compliance
Lightning Source LLC
LaVergne TN
LVHW051700050326
832903LV00032B/3923